Nick Vandome

Digital SLR Photography

Second Edition

In easy steps is an imprint of In Easy Steps Limited
Southfield Road · Southam
Warwickshire CV47 0FB · United Kingdom
www.ineasysteps.com

Second Edition

Notice of Liability
Every effort has been made to ensure that this book contains accurate
and current information. However, In Easy Steps Limited and the
author shall not be liable for any loss or damage suffered by readers
as a result of any information contained herein.

Trademarks
All trademarks are acknowledged as belonging to their respective
companies.

In Easy Steps Limited supports The Forest Stewardship Council (FSC),
the leading international forest certification organisation. All our titles
that are printed on Greenpeace approved FSC certified paper carry the
FSC logo.

Mixed Sources
Product group from well-managed
forests and other controlled sources
www.fsc.org Cert no. SGS-COC-005998
© 1996 Forest Stewardship Council

FSC

Printed and bound in the United Kingdom

ISBN 978-1-84078-437-4

Contents

4   Camera Techniques   65

5   Lighting Issues   77

6   Exposure and Metering   91

1 Around a Digital SLR

This chapter provides a thorough overview of digital SLR cameras and shows how they can be of great benefit to all photographers. It covers the construction of a digital SLR and the controls that you can expect to find on this type of camera. It also looks at issues relating to digital photography and covers some of the accessories that you may need to enhance your photography.

About This Book

The purpose of this book is simple: to explain the general workings of digital SLR cameras, show how to use them and also how to take better photographs with them. Hopefully, it will make you more confident about taking control with your digital SLR and begin to think more as a photographer rather than just as someone who takes a few snaps with a camera.

Taming the technology

Digital SLR cameras are complex in their design and consist of a remarkable amount of electrical and digital wizardry. However, the idea of this book is to give you enough technical information about digital SLRs so that you can use them effectively, without producing a dissertation about the finer points of the technology. The aim is to give you the technical information that you need to use a digital SLR without weighing you down with scientific formulae, charts and graphs. (Thousands of pages do exist with this type of detail, but this book concentrates on the practical rather than the theory.) The first three chapters of the book look at the workings of digital SLR cameras and how you can get the most out of using them.

Focusing on photography

The other main emphasis of the book is about using digital SLRs to take better photographs. When you feel comfortable about the functions of your camera you will be able to spend more time on capturing images.

Various shooting situations are looked at, with particular emphasis on the settings that can be used on a digital SLR.

The book is not a guide to editing images or image editing software (there are dozens of these on the market and two to look at are *Photoshop in easy steps* and *Photoshop Elements in easy steps*). Although image editing is a crucial part of digital photography it is always important to try and take the best photographs in the first place. This will reduce the need for extensive editing and just because you can take hundreds of images on a digital camera it does not mean that you should not strive to make each one as good as it possibly can be.

Ultimately, this book hopes to demystify the subject of digital SLR photography and help you to become a confident photographer who has fun and produces stunning images.

Why a Digital SLR?

When digital photography was in its infancy, the concept of digital SLR (Single Lens Reflex) cameras was something of an unobtainable dream for most photographers. However, times change quickly in the digital world and digital SLRs are now a credible, and affordable, option for anyone who wants to expand their photographic horizons.

History

The first digital SLR camera to significantly make an impact on the consumer market was the Canon EOS 300D (also known as the Digital Rebel). Released in August 2003 this was the first truly affordable digital SLR. It also achieved a level of quality that made a lot of photographers sit up and pay attention to the possibilities of digital SLRs. The EOS 300D was quickly followed by the Nikon D70 and these two manufacturers still command the majority of the digital SLR market, with approximately 40% each. Other players in the digital SLR market include Olympus, Sony, Pentax, Fujifilm, Mamiya, Sigma and Leica.

Advantages

Since the introduction of the EOS 300D, digital SLRs have made huge advances, in terms of both quality and affordability. When considering whether to buy a digital SLR, some areas to look at are:

- **Quality.** Digital SLR cameras provide better image quality than compact digital cameras, generally through the use of a larger image sensor for capturing images. (This is why a digital SLR will capture a higher quality image than a compact digital camera with the same pixel count.) Even if you always keep a digital SLR in automatic mode it will consistently capture images of the highest quality

- **Functionality.** When affordable digital SLR cameras first came onto the market, a lot of photographers were disparaging about them, claiming that they did not have the quality or functionality of traditional film SLR cameras. However, as the quality has increased so has the functionality, to the point where there is little difference between the digital and the film versions. This functionality gives you the flexibility to take greater control over your photography

Don't forget

Digital SLR cameras have detachable lenses which is one reason why they offer a lot more flexibility than compact cameras.

Don't forget

Websites such as Amazon now have dedicated sections for digital SLR cameras.

- **Pixels.** Since the advent of digital photography, most users have become familiar with the words 'pixels' and 'megapixels'. A contraction of 'picture element', pixels are the tiny colored dots that are used to create digital images. Digital cameras are referred to as having a resolution of a certain number of pixels (e.g. 10 million) or a megapixel value (e.g. 10 megapixels). A megapixel is equivalent to one million pixels. In general, digital SLRs have a higher pixel count than compact varieties, with figures currently moving up towards 15 million for some manufacturers. The pixels in a digital SLR tend to also be of a higher quality since their image sensors are larger than their compact counterparts. This enables more color information to be captured for each individual pixel, resulting in a higher quality image

- **Price.** The days of digital SLRs being prohibitively expensive have thankfully passed and in a lot of cases it is a question of which digital SLR camera to buy rather than whether to buy one. Most manufacturers have an entry level camera and then a range of more sophisticated, and expensive, models. The entry level models usually offer exceptional quality and enough functionality for most amateur photographers and they are an excellent option for anyone taking their first steps in the world of digital SLR photography

- **Speed.** One of the great technical advantages of digital SLR cameras is their speed. This covers: start up time, shot time lag and shot recycling speed. Start up time refers to the time it takes the camera to be ready for use once it is turned on. Since compact digital cameras rely on a lot of digital wizardry just to be ready for use, their start up time is a lot longer than a digital SLR, which is ready for use almost immediately. Shot time lag is the fraction of a second that elapses in compact cameras from when the shutter release button is pressed to when the photo is captured. This small delay can result in an unsatisfactory final image but the operation of a digital SLR ensures that the image is captured as soon as the shutter release button is pressed. Shot recycling speed refers to how long it takes a digital camera to be ready to take the next photo; in most digital SLRs it is almost immediate

Don't forget

Image sensors and pixel quality are something that digital SLR manufacturers are constantly looking to improve in terms of both size and quality.

Camera Body

One of the essential differences between a digital SLR camera and the compact alternative is that the SLR has two distinct elements: the camera body and the lens. The camera body contains all of the necessary functionality for the camera, while the lenses are used to transfer light through to the camera body and the image sensor, where the image is captured.

Digital SLR camera bodies can be bought separately from lenses but they are frequently sold together and you can also buy a digital SLR camera kit, which usually consists of the camera body and two lenses.

Feel

The first thing to consider about the camera body is how it actually feels in your hands, since camera bodies differ in terms of size and materials. It is important that you feel comfortable handling the camera as it could become an irritation if you do not feel at ease with the body. Pay particular attention to the grip as this will be the main point that you use to keep the camera steady.

Weight

The weight of a digital SLR is another factor that you should take into consideration. By their nature they are larger, and heavier, than compact cameras and this is something else that you should physically test before you buy one. In general, entry level digital SLRs are lighter than more sophisticated models and cameras from different manufacturers can also vary in weight. Consider the weight in relation to using the camera and also carrying it around – once you have added a couple of lenses and a good quality camera bag you may find that your digital SLR package weighs a lot more than just the camera body. Of course, some users will favor a more substantial feel as it can be more reassuring.

Controls

The functionality of the standard controls of digital SLRs are largely consistent across different models. The controls are usually dials and buttons situated on the camera body that are used to access the most commonly used functions of the camera (see the facing page for details). As with the feel and weight of the camera, it is important to test these controls to ensure that you can access them quickly and easily. If you are in a pressurized shooting situation you want to make sure that you do not have to spend a lot of time fiddling around with the controls.

Beware

Even if you are buying a digital SLR camera online, take the time to physically test the same model before you buy it.

12

Don't forget

The camera body is also where the batteries are housed. The best type to use are rechargeable Lithium batteries, known as Lithium-Ion.

Controls

Although digital SLRs have extensive menu systems (see next page) they also have a number of controls on the camera body, in the form of dials and buttons. This replicates the design of film SLR cameras and allows the user to quickly access the most frequently used functions of the camera. The types of controls that are found on digital SLRs are:

Control wheel

This is used to access shooting modes such as preset modes and other settings such as aperture priority, shutter priority, automatic and fully manual.

Focus selection

This is used to select the method of focus, usually autofocus or manual focus.

Metering

This is used to select the method of metering a scene to determine the required exposure. The options are usually matrix metering, center-weighted metering and spot metering.

Exposure compensation

This is used to increase or decrease the amount of light in a scene.

Flash

This is used to activate the camera's onboard flash unit.

Shooting mode

This is used to select whether to use the camera in single shot mode, self timer or continuous shooting mode i.e. shots keep being taken for as long as the shutter release button is held down.

ISO

This is used to change the camera's ISO equivalent settings. This is used to make the image sensor more, or less, sensitive to light. It is used in different lighting conditions and is looked at in more detail in Chapter Two.

White balance

This is used to change the camera's white balance settings. It is used to maintain image consistency when taking photos under different types of light i.e. sunlight, cloud, artificial light and flash. This is looked at in more detail in Chapter Five.

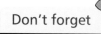

Don't forget

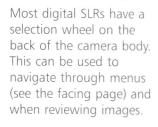

Most digital SLRs have a selection wheel on the back of the camera body. This can be used to navigate through menus (see the facing page) and when reviewing images.

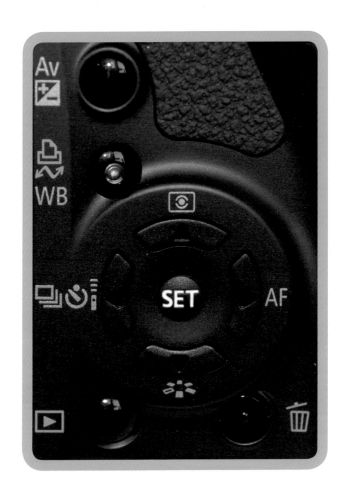

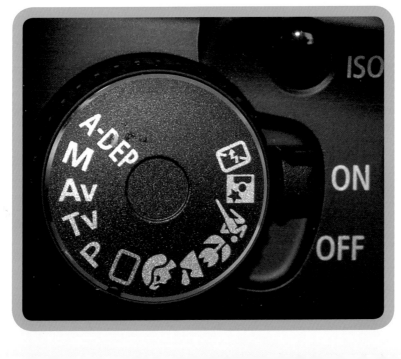

Menus

In addition to the camera controls, digital SLRs have a wealth of options within the camera menus. These are accessed through the Menu button (usually situated on the back of the camera body, next to the LCD screen) and are viewed on the LCD screen. Each camera menu system will have separate sections, with various selection options in each section.

Accessing and navigating menus

Camera menus can usually be accessed by pressing the Menu button on the back of the camera:

Don't forget

Depending on the manufacturer, some digital SLR cameras may have more than one series of menus for each option i.e. there may be two shooting menus.

Once within the menu structure, it is possible to navigate around it with the selection wheel:

Move up and down the menus by pressing the vertical buttons and through a menu option by pressing the horizontal buttons.

Shooting menus

These include options for:

- Image optimization

- Image quality

- Image size

- ISO settings

- White balance settings

- Noise reduction

- Image sharpening

- Hue and contrast

Play (Playback) menus

These include options for:

- Deleting images

- Image orientation on screen

- Slideshow options

- Printing options

- Protecting images from deletion

- Folder selection options

Setup menus

These include options for:

- Formatting memory cards

- Date and time

- Language

- Screen display information

- File numbering

- Auto shooting information

- Video options (if available)

Customizable menus

These menus can be used to create your own custom settings that can be applied for certain shooting situations.

Retouch menus

These include options for:

- Red-eye reduction

- Crop

- Special effects

Help menus

These offer help information about the functions of the camera and also for photographic situations.

Viewfinder and LCD Screen

Composing a scene and reviewing the results are essential parts of a digital camera. For digital SLRs, the former has traditionally been done by the viewfinder and the latter by the LCD screen. However, in recent years a new technology has been developed to enable the LCD screen to be used to compose an image too. This is known as live view and is looked at on page 20.

Viewfinder

The viewfinder of a digital SLR is the small window through which you look to compose a scene. It contains information about the current camera settings and it also enables you to select features such as the point of focus in a scene. The important issue to remember with a viewfinder on a digital SLR is to go for an optical one rather than an electric one; optical viewfinders give a more accurate image and this is one case when the old fashioned method is better than the technological one.

LCD screen

Traditionally, the LCD (Liquid Crystal Display) screen on a digital SLR has been used for three main reasons:

- Reviewing images that have been taken. This can be used to display a variety of information about the images, such as the camera settings used when the image was captured. The magnification can also be increased to view image details

- Menu settings. Other than camera body controls, the menu options of a digital SLR are accessed and displayed through the LCD screen

- Camera settings. Some digital SLRs display the current camera settings on the LCD screen. This is a more recent development (in earlier digital SLRs this information was usually shown in a small window on the top of the camera body) and is an excellent way to quickly see the settings for a particular shot

Due to their design, digital SLR cameras have not historically lent themselves to using the LCD panel as an additional viewfinder in the same way as compact digitals do. However, in 2006 the first digital SLR with this feature (known as live view) appeared and it is now widely available.

Don't forget

Camera setting information on the LCD screen includes: information about the aperture, shutter speed, white balance setting, ISO setting, focus area, exposure settings and battery charge level.

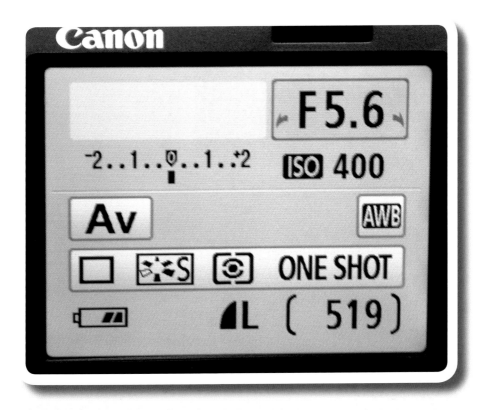

Live View

One of the recent innovations for digital SLR cameras has been the introduction of live view as a means of framing a scene before the image is captured. Users of compact digital cameras will be very familiar with this technology; almost all compacts use live view as the means of displaying a scene, done via the LCD screen. However, it was not until 2008 that this started to appear regularly on digital SLR cameras.

How it works

Due to their design digital SLR cameras show an accurate, optical, image of a scene in the camera's viewfinder. This is done through a series of mirrors in the camera and the lens, which produces an accurate representation of what is seen through the viewfinder. However, compact digital cameras do not have the luxury of this type of design and so have to rely on other methods for framing a scene. One way to do this is live view. This is often achieved by projecting a continuous image from the lens onto the image sensor. The LCD screen can then be used to view this continuous projection. The projection is achieved through electronic, rather than optical, means and so is not as accurate as an optical viewfinder.

Why live view on a digital SLR?

In some ways the existence of live view on digital SLRs is something that has been done just because it is possible. The optical viewfinder is still more accurate and there are two advantages of using this over live view:

- **Functionality.** Due to the fact that live view relies on complicated electronic technology this restricts its functionality. In particular, there are issues around the use of autofocus and using some of the camera's different shooting modes. It also uses more battery power

- **Steadiness.** If you are using live view with a digital SLR then the camera body and lens will be held at a distance from your body, unlike using the optical viewfinder. This increases the possibility of a blurred image due to camera shake, i.e. the camera moving slightly as the shot is being taken

Live view is an interesting development but one that has a long way to go until it regularly challenges the optical viewfinder.

Don't forget

Different makes of digital SLRs have different ways of accessing the live view option. Some perform it through the camera's menu system (see facing page) while others do it through a button on the camera body.

Hot tip

Uses for live view include close-up shots where you may not be able to get your eye next to the viewfinder or for portrait shots where you may want to talk to the subject without looking through the viewfinder.

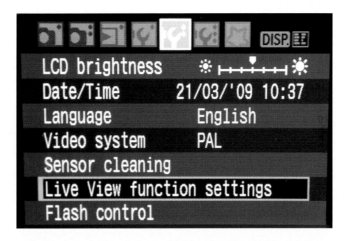

LCD brightness ☀ ┝━━━▼━━━┥ ☀
Date/Time   21/03/'09 10:37
Language   English
Video system   PAL
Sensor cleaning
Live View function settings
Flash control

Live View function settings

Live View shoot.   Enable
Grid display   Off
Metering timer   16 sec.

125   9.0 ⁻2..1..▼..1..⁺2   [572] ISO 200

Memory Cards

Memory cards are devices for storing digital images once they have been captured by the camera. They come in several types and sizes, with the main ones being:

- Compact Flash
- SD (Secure Digital) and SDHC
- Memory Stick
- SmartMedia
- xD Picture Card

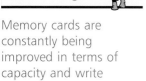

Don't forget

Memory cards are constantly being improved in terms of capacity and write speeds, i.e. how quickly data can be written from the camera.

Some memory cards are specific to a certain camera manufacturer (e.g. the Memory Stick is a Sony product) while others can be used across different makes of camera.

The most widely used type of memory card is the Compact Flash type. This is also the largest memory card, which is not as much of an issue for digital SLRs as it is for compacts, due to the former's larger size. However, the smaller SD and SDHC cards are becoming increasingly common in digital SLRs, as manufacturers seek to save space for other features and also reduce weight.

Memory cards come in a selection of different storage sizes. However, due to the increased file size of images taken with a digital SLR, always go for the largest-capacity card that you can afford. At the time of writing, memory cards of 16 GB are available and a minimum of 4 GB is a reasonable option (the cost of memory cards has fallen dramatically since they were first introduced).

Another issue to consider with memory cards is the speed at which they write image data from the camera. This also depends on your camera's processor and the file format you are using to capture images. The faster the card the better, as this will enable you to capture the next image more quickly.

Memory cards should be treated carefully and always make sure you carry a spare one, in case you fill up a card while you are shooting and do not have time to download your images. To insert a memory card, open the relevant compartment on your camera and push it firmly into place, making sure that it is inserted the right way.

Image Sensors

In all digital cameras, the image sensor is the equivalent of the film in a traditional 35mm camera. One of the crucial differences between a compact digital camera and a digital SLR is the size, and quality, of the image sensor. Since the body of a digital SLR is larger than a compact, this allows for larger sensors to be used. This produces a higher quality as higher numbers of pixels can be captured and the individual pixels can also be larger. This means that they can store more color information. However, despite this, most image sensors are still not as large as 35mm film, so the area for capturing the image is still smaller than the traditional analog method.

How they work

An image sensor is a complex and sensitive piece of electronic circuitry. It consists of a microchip onto which is placed thousands of photosites. These contain photodiodes that capture the light that falls on the sensor and converts it into an electrical charge. This charge is then converted into a digital file and processed by the camera into the final image. To produce the color in the image, the sensor uses filters to convert the light into elements of red, blue and green. This is then used to mix all of the other colors in the image. All of this requires an array of sophisticated technology, which is managed by the camera's processor.

Types of sensors

As with a lot of areas of technology, there is no single standard for image sensors. The two main types are CMOS (Complementary Metal Oxide Semiconductor) and CCD (Charge Coupled Device). They both have their own merits but ultimately there is very little to choose between the two in terms of image quality. Different camera manufacturers favor one type of image sensor or another, but this should not influence your decision to buy a particular camera.

- **CMOS.** These sensors are produced in a similar way to standard computer elements so they are generally cheaper to make. They also use less power and are slightly faster at transferring data

- **CCD.** These sensors are slightly more expensive to produce and although they are an analog device that converts each individual pixel they have a similar performance to CMOS

Don't forget

There are other image sensors on the market, such as the Foveon X3. This uses photodiodes that capture red, green and blue color values, rather than just one. This is known as full-color image capture and can create a higher quality image.

File Formats

A file format is a way of creating a digital image once the light and color information has been captured by the image sensor and then converted into digital data by the processor. This is also known as digital encoding and there are dozens of possible ways in which this can be done. However, digital photography has firmly adopted three formats:

- JPEG (Joint Photographic Experts Group)

- TIFF (Tagged Image File Format)

- RAW

Don't forget

JPEG and TIFF images are compatible across different image editing programs and so are very flexible in terms of sharing with other people and viewing on different computers.

These three file formats all offer different advantages in terms of compression, file size, versatility and image quality.

JPEG

JPEG is a file format that was developed to display digital images on the Web. The reason for this is that JPEG images can be compressed into relatively small file sizes. Although this compression results in some loss of image quality, it is not always visible to the naked eye, particularly on the Web. Because of the loss of image quality, the JPEG file format is known as using "lossy compression". JPEGs use the .jpg file extension e.g. nick.jpg.

JPEG is the most commonly used file format for digital images and it is an excellent option for digital SLR users, particularly if you want to store more images on a memory card. The quality of JPEG images is also generally very good.

TIFF

The TIFF file format also uses compression to reduce the file size of the final image. However, it uses a lossless form of compression, which means that no image quality is lost when compression takes place. This is done most commonly by using the LZW (Lempel-Ziv-Welch) method of compression (when working with TIFF images in an image editing program the compression method can be selected when the edited image is being saved). This creates higher quality images and also larger file sizes than JPEGs. TIFF images are often used to achieve the best print quality for digital images and they can readily be transferred between different users. Unlike JPEGs, TIFFs can be edited numerous times without losing image quality. TIFFs use the .tif file extension e.g. nick.tif.

RAW

As the name suggests, the RAW file format is one where there is very little editing done to the digital data captured by the camera i.e. it is still in its raw state. When both JPEGs and TIFFs are created there is a lot of digital editing applied to them in terms of compression, white balance, hue and contrast and other similar elements. However, with RAW images all of these elements can be edited by the user with an image editing program. All of this information is stored separately from the image so it is possible to edit the image data as it was captured. Most professional photographers shoot in the RAW format as it gives ultimate control over the final image and the highest quality. In many ways the RAW format can be considered as the 'digital negative'.

Each camera manufacturer uses its own proprietary format for RAW images. The file extensions for these include:

- .nef for Nikon RAW

- .crw for Canon RAW

- .orf for Olympus RAW

- .pef for Pentax RAW

- .srf for Sony RAW

Despite these different formats for RAW they can all be opened in software programs that support RAW. Attempts have been made by Adobe to standardize the format, with their Digital Negative (DNG) offering, but this has met with limited success.

The main reason for using the RAW format is so that you can take full control over the editing process. RAW is not a format for outputting edited images; at this point the file has to be saved as a JPEG, a TIFF or another file format.

When editing RAW files you need an image editing program that supports this. The industry standard is Adobe Photoshop and this is the best option if you are going to be doing a lot of work in RAW. For Mac users, who do not want to use the Mac version of Photoshop, the Aperture program offers a similar service. In addition, a lot of other programs now have RAW plug-ins for viewing and editing RAW files.

Resolution

The term resolution is one that is used frequently in the world of digital photography and it can refer to several different areas of the process: image size, viewing size and print size. For digital cameras themselves, resolution refers to the size, in number of pixels, of the images that can be captured by the camera.

Digital cameras are frequently referred to in terms of their resolution i.e. 12 million pixels or 12 megapixels. This denotes the total number of pixels in an image and the figure used by manufacturers usually refers to the resolution for the camera at its highest setting. For instance a digital SLR that can capture an image at 4200 x 2800 will have a resolution of approximately 12 million pixels.

Resolution settings

Most digital SLR cameras have at least three resolution settings, which can be accessed from the Shooting Menu, under the heading of Resolution or Image Size. Changing this setting physically alters the number of pixels that are captured for an image. The settings are usually Small, Medium or Large. Obviously, the larger the number of pixels in an image, the greater the resultant file size once it has been captured.

Which resolution?

Since resolution affects an image's size and quality the issue of which resolution you should use is one that should be settled before you start shooting. The main question is whether you want to print the image or display it on a computer. For print, a higher number of pixels is required for a good quality image so the highest resolution should be used; for displaying on a computer a lower number of pixels will suffice so a lower resolution can be used. However, to be on the safe side it is usually best to capture all of your images at the highest resolution and then reduce them in size within a program such as Photoshop, if you want to put them to different uses. This involves removing some of the pixels from the image. Pixels can also be added to an image to increase its size but it is always best to capture it at the highest resolution in the first place, if possible.

Don't forget

When looking at the resolution of a digital SLR camera make sure that you check the specifications for the effective pixel count. This is the actual number of pixels that are in the final image. For most cameras a small number of pixels are used for processing purposes, even though they are included in the headline figure in terms of resolution.

Image Size

The issue of image size is a close relation to resolution and it determines the size at which an image is displayed within its selected media. Generally, for printed images the largest image size is best, while images that are going to be used on the Web can be of a smaller size.

As a rule, the size (in inches) at which images can be printed is calculated by dividing the number of pixels (horizontal and vertical values) by 300. This means that the printed image will use 300 pixels for every inch of the final output. This is known as the image resolution. For instance, the image example on the previous page could be printed at a size of 14 inches by 9.3 inches i.e. 4200 pixels divided by 300 and 2800 divided by 300.

For images that are going to be used on the Web, the pixel dimensions are divided by 96 (as this is the general resolution of computer monitors) to give the image size. For the example above this would give an approximate size of 42 inches by 28 inches. Obviously, this would be far too large for use on the Web. To overcome this, you could select a lower resolution when capturing the image. Alternatively, the image could be captured at its largest size and then reduced in an image editing program such as Photoshop. This can be done by changing the values in the Image Size window. The number of pixels can be reduced by changing the values in the Pixel Dimensions section.

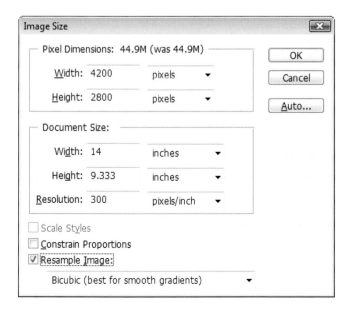

Lenses

After the body, the other primary element of a digital SLR is the lens or, in a lot of cases, lenses. The ability to change lenses on a digital SLR is one of the key features for photographers as it enables them to use different lenses for different shooting conditions. The types of available lenses are:

- **Fixed.** These are lenses with a fixed focal length i.e. 50mm. These offer less flexibility than zoom lenses but they usually provide higher quality at the specific focal length

- **Zoom.** These are lenses that have a range of focal length i.e. 18-55mm, or 70-210mm. They are good all-round lenses

- **Wide-angle.** These are lenses that can capture a very wide viewing area. This can be effective for landscape photography. Some extremely wide-angle lenses are known as fisheye lenses

- **Macro.** These are speciality lenses that enable you to get very close to objects

- **Telephoto.** These are fixed focal length lenses that offer a high level of magnification

Due to the fact that most image sensors within digital cameras are smaller than the equivalent film this means that the level of magnification of lenses is greater than for a film SLR camera. As a general rule of thumb the focal length of a lens on a digital SLR can be increased by 50% to get the equivalent for the same lens being used on a film camera. For instance, as 50mm lens is equivalent to a 75mm one on a film camera and a 200mm one is equivalent to a 300mm one. This is good news for zoom lenses as the image is magnified more on a digital SLR. However, it is not so good if you want to achieve a very wide angle – an 18mm lens would give you an equivalent focal length of 27mm, which reduces the viewing area considerably.

The other consideration with lenses is their speed. This is the speed at which they let light through the aperture. The faster this happens the better, as it gives you greater flexibility for adjusting the aperture/shutter speed combination. Lens speeds are denoted by their f-numbers and the lower the better. So an f2 lens will be faster, and more expensive, than an equivalent lens that has an f-number of f4.5.

Don't forget

The higher the focal length, the narrower the viewing area and the greater the magnification of the subject or scene.

28

Don't forget

Look for lenses that have anti-shake technology. This is designed to create a sharper, crisper image. Generally it is used on longer, larger lenses that are more likely to suffer from camera shake due to movement of the lens.

Flash

Flash is the method of providing additional lighting to a scene when there is not sufficient natural light. It can be overused, particularly if a camera is set to automatic and activates the flash whenever it thinks there is insufficient light. Digital SLRs offer a lot more flexibility for avoiding having to use flash if you do not want to, such as extensive ISO settings for low level lighting.

But when you do need to use flash, digital SLRs can be equipped to produce very sophisticated results.

On-camera flash

Almost all digital SLR cameras have some form of on-camera flash. This is usually a pop-up unit on top of the camera body, which is usually activated by a button on the body. These types of flash units do not always look very powerful or robust but they can have a surprisingly effective output and are sufficient for a number of flash uses. The main drawback with on-camera flash units is that they are fixed and so can only provide a direct, frontal light, which limits the creative uses for the flash. This type of flash invariably leaves shadows in unwanted areas of the image.

Detachable flash

Detachable flash units are more powerful and flexible than on-camera flash and they should be considered seriously if you intend to make regular use of flash. Detachable units are attached via the hotshoe on the top of the camera body and they are powered by their own batteries (always keep a spare set handy). The advantages of a detachable flash unit are:

- They are more powerful and flexible than an on-camera flash

- The head can be swivelled so that the flash does not fire directly at the subject. A common way to use this is to 'bounce' the flash off a flat surface, such as a ceiling. When doing this, try and use a smooth, bright surface, otherwise some of the light may be absorbed rather than bounced. Using flash in this way gives a more even effect, particularly for portraits, and it is a good way to remove shadows from behind a subject

- More accurate color temperature. This means that the white balance when using flash is better than with an on-camera flash unit

Beware

If you are using the on-camera flash for portrait photographs then the subject is more likely to suffer from 'red-eye'. A detachable flash is more effective as you can bounce the flash so that it is not aimed directly at the subject.

Tripods

A good quality tripod is more important for a digital SLR camera than a compact one. There are two reasons for this:

- Since digital SLRs, and their lenses, are heavier than compacts there will be occasions where you will need to keep the camera steady for long periods of time, e.g. if you are taking photographs of wildlife

- Due to the functionality of a digital SLR there will be more opportunities to use slower shutter speeds to achieve certain creative effects. This could be to capture images of scenes at night (such as illuminated buildings or fireworks) or to create a sense of motion with items such as water or vehicles. If you are altering the shutter speed of your camera, anything slower than 1/60th of a second should be shot using a tripod. Otherwise the shutter speed will be too slow for you to hold the camera perfectly steady, resulting in camera shake that can cause the image to appear blurry

Testing a tripod

As with digital SLR cameras themselves, it is always a good idea to physically test a variety of tripods before you buy one. Some areas to look at are:

- **Stability.** This is a crucial factor and buying a cheaper, flimsier tripod could be a false economy. Press down on the head of the tripod and also twist the head both ways. The tripod should remain in place without any movement or vibration. (Bear in mind that you will probably be using the tripod outside so it has to remain stable even in windy conditions)

- **Type of head.** The head is the attachment to which the camera is fixed. The three main types are ball, three-way and two-way. A ball head gives the most versatility while a three-way head probably gives the most overall control. Whichever type of head you choose, it is important that you are comfortable with it and can make adjustments quickly so that you do not miss any shots

- **Weight.** If you are going to be carrying a tripod then its weight could be an issue. Usually you will have to make a judgement between price, stability and weight

Beware

An increased focal length (e.g. when using a zoom lens) not only increases the magnification of the scene, it also makes the camera more prone to camera shake. Therefore always consider using a tripod with a very high focal length lens, i.e. 300mm or above.

Cleaning

After water, dust is the greatest threat to the delicate electronic circuitry of digital SLR cameras. The image sensor is the most precious element in terms of protection from dust and any other small, unwanted objects. Unfortunately two factors conspire against digital SLRs in terms of dust:

- The electronics within the cameras can help attract dust particles

- When changing lenses the camera body is open to the elements. Although the sensor is not directly exposed, it does increase the possibility that dust particles could find their way onto the image sensor

If dust does settle on the image sensor this can result in small spots on the resultant images. These can be removed in image editing software, but it is better to try and avoid this in the first instance, if possible.

Manufacturers of digital SLRs are well aware of the issue of dust and take considerable steps to try and alleviate the problem. They all have a variety of methods to try and reduce the amount of dust that is attracted to the sensor. These include low-pass filters covering the sensor, anti-static coatings on vulnerable surfaces and screens in front of the sensor that stop any particles.

Removing dust

If dust particles do attach themselves to the image sensor to a degree that it is a significant problem there are two options:

- Use a reputable camera repair shop to professionally remove the dust

- Remove the dust yourself. To do this, first access the camera's setup menu and select the option to lock the camera's mirror into the Up position. (This will provide you with access to the camera's image sensor, see facing page) Then, shine a bright torch onto the sensor. This should reveal the dust particle. If necessary, use a magnifying glass to see the dust particle more clearly. Use a hand-powered bulb blower to remove the dust particle. If this is too weak a can of compressed air can be used but since this is more powerful it also carries a risk of damaging other elements within the camera

Hot tip

When changing lenses, try and do it in an environment that is as dust free as possible and, ideally, with no wind. In reality this is not always possible, and if you are in windy conditions, use a jacket, or similar, to offer some protection.

Beware

If using a can of compressed air to clean an image sensor, use it from a few inches away and hold the can level. Never physically touch the sensor as this may damage it permanently.

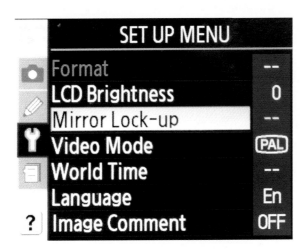

SET UP MENU

Format		--
LCD Brightness		0
Mirror Lock-up		--
Video Mode		PAL
World Time		--
Language		En
Image Comment		OFF

Mirror Lock-up (cleaning)

When shutter button is pressed, mirror lifts and shutter opens. To lower mirror, turn camera off.

Filters

Another area in which digital SLR cameras have an advantage over compacts is through the use of filters. These are discs that are placed over the end of the lens to create a variety of effects. Generally, these are used to alter one, or more, of the lighting conditions in an image. These effects can be used subtly to improve the overall quality of the image, or more dramatically to create a more obvious special effect.

Filters can be attached to lenses with a dedicated lens holder attachment or they can be screwed onto the end of the lens.

Types of filters

The types of filters most commonly used on digital SLRs are:

- **Ultraviolet (UV).** These are clear filters that are used to remove any haziness caused by ultraviolet light. They have no other effect on incoming light and are frequently used as a means of protecting the front of the lens. In general, a UV filter can be kept on the front of the lens at all times

- **Polarizing.** These are filters that cut out polarized light. They are frequently used to make skies look darker or to cut out reflections from surfaces such as glass or water. Polarizing filters can either be linear or circular, but both produce a similar effect

- **Graduated.** These are filters that are graduated to help balance out the difference between the darkest (shadows) and lightest (highlights) areas in an image. These filters can be neutral or come in different colors. They are particularly useful for enhancing the sky

- **Diffusion.** These are filters that can be used to soften a subject by creating a hazy effect over the image. Diffusion filters are frequently used in portrait photography to create a soft, dream-like effect. Some diffusion filters have a clear area in the center of the lens so that the main subject is clearer and the background is softened

2 Functionality of a D-SLR

Digital SLRs offer a lot more flexibility than compact cameras and this chapter details the functionality that can be used to achieve this.

Aperture

Although digital SLRs can be used as high quality 'point and shoot' cameras, this does not begin to exploit their full range of functionality. This functionality helps to give you more control over the images that you capture and you can begin to choose the way in which a certain scene appears.

One of the most fundamental controls that a digital SLR camera gives you is aperture priority.

In photographic terms, aperture describes the opening in a lens through which light passes on its way to be captured on the camera's image sensor. A diaphragm is used to create a gap to control the amount of light passing through the lens. A large gap allows a lot of light to pass through the lens, while a smaller gap restricts the amount of light passing through. Each degree of opening is known as an aperture stop and is usually denoted by an f-number (this is the ratio of the focal length of the lens to the diameter of the aperture). A small f-number (e.g. f2.8) denotes a wide aperture (i.e. a lot of light can pass through) while a large f-number (e.g. f22) denotes a narrow aperture (i.e. a smaller amount of light can pass through).

The significance of aperture is that it affects the overall exposure of an image i.e. how much light is captured by the image sensor. Obviously, this is crucial to how the final image appears: too much light and it will be too bright (over-exposed), too little light and it will be too dark (under-exposed). The other significant element in exposure is shutter speed (i.e. how long the shutter in the lens remains open to let light pass through).

It is the combination of aperture and shutter speed that determines how much light is captured by the image sensor. When a camera is set to automatic, it calculates the correct aperture and shutter speed in order to exposure the image correctly. However, this does not allow for much flexibility from the photographer's point of view. This is where aperture priority comes into play. This allows the photographer to set a specific aperture and the camera will then select the required shutter speed for the correct exposure. The main reason for doing this is for the photographic technique known as depth of field.

Don't forget

The aperture for each shot will be shown on your camera's main display. If you have set the aperture yourself (i.e. aperture priority) it will remain the same even if you recompose the scene. However, in automatic mode the aperture will change each time the scene is recomposed, as the camera tries to set the required exposure settings for the scene.

Depth of Field

The depth of field in an image is the area in front of and behind the subject that remains in focus. Depth of field is an important consideration if you want to have a subject that is sharply in focus while the background is blurred.

This can be an effective technique because it gives more prominence to the main subject in the image. If the image is captured with a larger depth of field then the main subject gets slightly lost in the background. This can be particularly distracting if the background is multi-colored or it contains numerous different items.

Depth of field is altered by changing the aperture setting on a camera: the wider the aperture (e.g. f2.8) then the less the depth of field i.e. the area of the image that remains in focus is reduced. The narrower the aperture (e.g. f22) the greater the depth of field i.e. more of the image will be in focus. Another way to change the depth of field is to move yourself, or your subject, so that there is a greater distance between the subject and the background.

Aperture priority is set by selecting the A option (Av on Canon digital SLRs) on your camera's control wheel. The aperture can then usually be changed by turning a dial on the camera body:

Don't forget

A large depth of field can be used for landscapes to ensure as much of the subject as possible is in focus.

Don't forget

For more information about using depth of field see Chapter Six.

Shutter Speed

As shown on the previous pages, the aperture on a digital SLR can be used to take control over depth of field. In a similar way, the shutter speed can be used to control motion (either by using a very fast shutter speed to freeze it, or a slow shutter speed to blur an element in an image) or to capture images in low level lighting.

Shutter speed priority mode is used by setting the camera controls to the S option (Tv on Canon digital SLRs). This enables you to set a specific shutter speed and the camera will select the appropriate aperture for the correct exposure. Digital SLR cameras have a significant range of shutter speeds, from 30 seconds to 1/8000th of a second. Faster shutter speeds are used for freezing motion, such as sporting events, or stopping water, while longer shutter speeds are used for situations where you need to blur a scene or capture a scene in low level lighting and you cannot, or do not want to, use flash, such as for fireworks.

Generally, for a shutter speed slower than 1/60th of a second a tripod should be used to keep the camera steady and avoid 'camera shake'. This occurs when the shutter is open for too long and the movement of your hand causes a blurry effect in the final image. Also, the larger the focal length of lens being used (e.g. a 300mm zoom lens) then the greater the likelihood of camera shake. If you can, use as fast a shutter speed as possible when using a large lens (or use a tripod).

Altering shutter speed

Once you have set the shutter speed this is displayed on the camera's LCD screen. When the camera is in shutter speed priority mode, the shutter speed can usually be altered by turning one of the dials on the camera body.

When a camera is set to shutter speed priority mode the shutter speed remains constant and the aperture changes depending on the scene that is being viewed. For instance, if it is a bright day the aperture will be fairly small (a high f-number — f16 in the top image on the facing page) as less light will be required. Conversely the aperture will increase (a lower f-number — f4.5 in the bottom image on the facing page) if it is a darker scene. To check this, compose two scenes with differing lighting conditions and see how the aperture changes (the shutter speed will always stay the same in shutter speed priority mode).

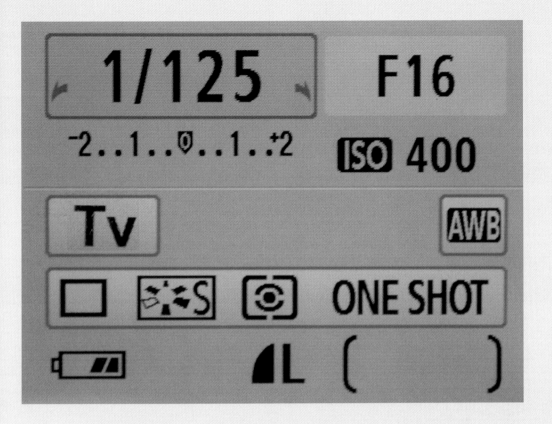

Understanding Exposure

Light is a crucial element in photography and exposure is the term used to describe the amount of light that is captured by the image sensor for a particular scene. As shown on the previous pages this is calculated by a combination of aperture and shutter speed. Different combinations can be used to achieve the same overall exposure, depending how you want to use the aperture and shutter speed.

The correct exposure for a digital photograph also depends on the sensitivity of the image sensor: the more sensitive the image sensor, the less light is required for the correct exposure. In the digital world this is generally known as the ISO equivalent. The higher the ISO number, the more sensitive the image sensor becomes (see overleaf).

Measuring exposure

Since exposure can be seen as a complex subject most compact digital cameras calculate the correct exposure and also make the corresponding settings for aperture and shutter speed. Although this usually creates excellent results, users of digital SLRs can take a lot more control of the process of measuring exposure.

The required exposure for a scene is calculated by taking light measurements from certain areas of the scene. Digital SLR cameras offer different ways of doing this:

- **Matrix metering (also known as multi-pattern metering).** This is usually the default metering option. It takes a light reading by dividing the scene into segments (usually 256) and taking a reading from each. These are then compared to a database of images with differing lighting conditions. Once this comparison has been made the exposure is set (top image)

- **Center-weighted metering.** This gives more emphasis to the area around the center of the image. It also includes light readings from other areas of the image (middle image)

- **Spot metering.** This type of metering takes a reading from a very small area in the center of the frame. This is the best way to obtain the correct exposure for a specific area of an image (bottom image)

Hot tip

A general photographic rule for estimating the correct exposure in normal daylight is known as the 'Sunny 16' rule. This works by setting the aperture to f16 and the shutter speed to match the ISO setting that you are using. So if it is a bright sunny day and you are using an ISO setting of 100, the exposure setting would be f16 at 1/100th of a second (on most cameras this is more likely to be 1/125th of a second).

ISO Settings

ISO settings (also known as film speed) is a term that has carried over from the world of film photography. It refers to how sensitive a certain type of film is to light. The more sensitive the film the less time it needs to be exposed to the light. The reason for ISO settings is so that photos can be captured in lower level light, by using a more sensitive type of film. The downside of this is that the image quality is reduced as the film sensitivity is increased.

Although the technology is different, digital photography has adopted the same ISO terminology (at times it is referred to as ISO equivalent settings). Digital SLR cameras have a wide range of ISO settings for image sensors: a standard range is 100–1600 (although more expensive models have a greater range still). The higher the ISO number, the less sensitive the image sensor is to light and so the exposure time can be reduced.

Some issues to be aware of in relation to ISO settings:

● At a low ISO setting (100 or 200) more light is required to create the correct exposure. This is therefore a good setting when light is not a major issue, such as a bright, sunny day

● At a high ISO setting (800 or above) less light is required to create the correct exposure. This is a good setting for low level lighting situations

● At higher ISO settings, the quality of the image is not as good as at a lower ISO setting. This is because the quality of the light is not as good and the camera is working harder to achieve the correct exposure. Especially in low level lighting this can cause 'noise' in the image. This is where the light is insufficient for the image sensor to capture the light detail accurately. This can result in randomly colored pixels appearing in the image. Noise is something that manufacturers of digital SLRs are working hard to reduce as much as possible. It is generally accepted that Canon digital SLRs perform the best in terms of high ISO numbers i.e. when capturing images in low level lighting

The images on the facing page show the same scene taken with different ISO settings (top image 400 ISO setting, bottom image 1600 ISO setting).

Don't forget

A lot of digital SLRs have Auto ISO settings. While this can be a good way to ensure you usually have enough light for a shot, it does not give you as much flexibility so it is usually better to set your own ISO and adjust the other controls accordingly.

Focal Length

Focal length can be thought of as the size of lens used for a particular shot. Since a lot of digital SLR cameras come with a least one zoom lens (usually in the range of approximately 18–55mm) this means that there are plenty of focal lengths from which to choose. The focal length is measured as the distance between the lens and the focal point i.e. where the image comes into focus. With a zoom lens the distance between the focal point and the lens changes as the focal length is altered.

Generally, a shorter focal length (e.g. 20mm) has a higher optical quality than a longer focal length. This is because there is a shorter distance between the lens and the focal point.

Angle of view

One of the main considerations with focal length is the angle of view. This is the area of a scene that is visible at a certain focal length. A short focal length will result in a large angle of view and a longer focal length will result in a more restricted angle of view. The images on the facing page show how the angle of view changes with the focal length.

For the majority of digital SLR cameras a focal length of approximately 50mm is equivalent to the angle of view of the human eye. This is sometimes referred to as a 1:1 focal length.

Don't forget

Lenses with a very short focal length e.g. 18mm are also known as 'fisheye' lenses, as this it the type of view that they create.

46

Focusing

Achieving an accurately focused image is a fundamental aspect of photography – if an image is out of focus then it is virtually unusable. Luckily, digital SLRs have a variety of options for dealing with focus.

Focusing methods

The two main methods of focus are manual and autofocus. Autofocus is the default method and this is achieved by the camera sending a laser beam to the subject and then calculating the focus accordingly. Once the autofocus has found the correct point it locks onto it, usually denoted by a solid green light in the viewfinder and, in some cases, an audible beep. If you do not want to use autofocus, or the conditions are not suitable for it, then manual focusing can be used. This is done by selecting the correct setting on the lens (usually done with a button on the lens: AF for Autofocus and MF [or M] for Manual Focus). Manual focus is then achieved by turning the focus ring at the front of the lens. By its nature, manual focus depends on the user's eyesight to achieve the correct degree of focus.

Hot tip

It is possible to turn off the 'beep' for autofocus confirmation. This can be done through the menu system, usually on the shooting menu.

Focus options

Within the autofocus functionality there are certain settings that can be selected. One of these is the different autofocus modes that can be used. These include:

- **Single shot mode.** This is best for inanimate subjects. Focus is achieved by half depressing the shutter release button and focus is set in one operation. The image can then be captured by fully depressing the shutter release button

- **AI Servo AF mode.** This is used for focusing on moving objects. When the shutter release button is half depressed the focus will keep readjusting for the moving object in the frame

- **AI Focus AF mode.** This is a combination of the above two modes. If the main subject is still, the camera will select Single Shot mode; if there is movement it will switch to AI Servo AF mode

Focus selection

When composing a scene it is not always the best creative option to have the main subject in the middle of the frame. Because of this digital SLRs offer various focus selection points i.e. you can choose to make the focal point in areas other than the center of the frame. Depending on the camera, usually seven, nine or eleven focal points can be selected from (see below). Focal points can be selected via the camera's menu or from the selection wheel on the camera body when the image is being composed.

Don't forget

Except in very low level lighting conditions autofocus is an excellent option for obtaining the correct focus. However, in low level lighting it can have problems finding areas of contrast on which to focus.

49

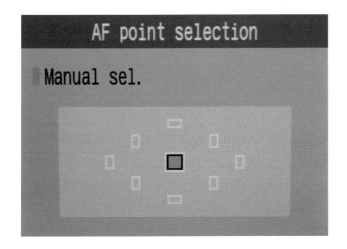

Automatic Settings

Even though digital SLR cameras afford a lot of control, including full manual control, they also have a variety of automatic settings that can be used for certain shooting conditions. These are not usually as extensive as compact cameras and for most digital SLR users they may have limited usefulness, particularly when you have become more confident about using the camera's functionality. However, they can be a good way of getting used to the settings for certain circumstances. For automatic settings, the camera will select the required aperture and shutter speed for the required style. In most cases, it will not be possible to change these settings manually. Automatic settings are usually accessed from the Mode dial on the top of the camera body.

Some automatic settings that are likely to be available on digital SLR cameras:

- **Portraits.** This mode creates a portrait with a blurred background, to give greater prominence to the main subject. This is done by setting a wide aperture and the shutter speed is selected accordingly

- **Landscapes.** This mode uses a wide aperture to ensure that as much of a landscape shot is in focus as possible

- **Close-ups.** This mode uses a wide aperture so that it creates a blurred background behind a subject captured in close-up. Ideally, a macro lens should be used when using this mode as it will enable you to get even closer to the subject

- **Moving objects.** This mode uses a fast shutter speed to freeze moving objects. It also activates AI Servo autofocus mode to focus on moving objects. It is very effective for areas such as sports photography

- **Night shots.** This can be used to create a balanced image in low level lighting. Use a tripod to ensure camera stability

Don't forget

The opposite of automatic settings is full Manual control. This is where the user selects the aperture and shutter speed themselves. Once this has been done they will not change while the shot is being composed. A scale in the viewfinder shows if the exposure for the scene is accurate or not. Manual control gives you the most control but it needs a bit of practice to become confident when using it.

3 Workflow

This chapter looks at what you can do once you have captured images with your camera. This includes looking at the workflow process and adding tags and keywords to images for searching purposes.

Why Workflow Matters

Don't forget

Everyone works differently so create your own workflow process and try and follow it every time you are working with digital images. This will enable you to achieve consistency in your work. See the end of this chapter for a sample workflow checklist.

Don't forget

A lot of computers now have internal card readers which makes it easier to download images from the card.

Capturing high quality images with a digital SLR is all very well, but it is what you do with them after this that is important. Workflow is a term to describe the process of downloading, storing, editing, tagging and outputting images once they have been captured. Ideally, you should have a workflow process in place for working with your digital images and try and follow it as consistently as possible. The importance of having a robust workflow process in place is that it will help you manage your images as your collection grows larger and larger.

Downloading

The first step in the workflow process is getting images from your digital SLR onto a computer. From here you can perform the rest of the workflow tasks. There are two main ways of transferring images from your camera:

- Via a cable connected to the camera and your computer

- Via a card reader, into which you place your camera's memory card and the reader is then connected to your computer like an external drive

Storing

When images have been downloaded they are stored on your computer's hard drive. However, once you have performed your workflow tasks it is essential that they are stored somewhere else too, for safekeeping. This can be in the form of an external hard drive or on CDs or DVDs

Tagging

Tagging is the process of adding keywords to images. This can be as simple or as complex as you want and it is used to locate images on your computer through a range of keywords.

Editing and outputting

There is a large range of image editing software on the market and this can be used to enhance and edit your images. Editing should always be included in the workflow process, even if you only use it minimally. Outputting involves optimizing images for printing or use on the Web, or both. In each case there is a different process that has to be followed in the workflow: larger, higher quality images have to be used for printing, while smaller ones can be used on the Web.

Computer Issues

While it is not absolutely essential to use a computer when working with digital images, it is highly recommended. If you are only interested in printing images then this can be done directly from the camera's memory card. However, anyone who is going to create a workflow process has to have a computer.

Windows PC or Mac

The two main types of computers on the market are PCs using Windows as their operating system and Apple Macs. Both have their pros and cons, but historically Macs have been considered more efficient at design related tasks. But both types of computers will do an excellent job of managing your digital images so it may come down to what you are used to, or the cost of the respective machines. For both, try and buy the newest model that you can.

Requirements

Most new computers currently on the market are well equipped to handle the workflow for digital images, in terms of processor speed and power and storage space. Some of the key areas to look at as far as your computer is concerned are:

Hot tip

Keep an eye out for upgrades to your computer's operating system and programs.

53

- **Monitor size.** Try and buy the largest and highest quality monitor that you can afford. If you are going to be working with digital images a lot then you will be spending a long time in front of your monitor. The bigger it is then the more of an individual image you will be able to view. Also, you will be able to arrange the programs for your workflow, such as image editing programs, more effectively

- **RAM (Random Access Memory).** This is the computer's memory that is used for handling open programs and dealing with editing requests. The more RAM the better as this makes your computer more stable and it also speeds up the editing process. This is an important factor as image editing can make significant demands on a computer's RAM. Aim for a minimum of 1GB of RAM

- **Backup storage.** Despite the fact that modern computers frequently come with a vast amount of storage space (hard drive space) it is essential that you have some form of external storage, so that you can back up your images. The best option is an external hard drive

Workflow Software

The market for workflow software is not as extensive as that for image editing but there are still some high quality and powerful products on the market. Two of the main ones are Photoshop Lightroom (for Windows PCs) and Aperture (Mac) and these are aimed at the serious amateur or professional photographers. However, they can also be used by anyone who wants to make sure that they have a robust workflow in place for their images. Some image editing programs also have some workflow elements such as image tagging and management. The best example of this is Photoshop Elements. Adobe Bridge is also a good option for managing collections of images.

Photoshop Lightroom

Photoshop Lightroom has been developed in recognition of the fact that tagging and organizing images is an essential function for a lot of photographs. Lightroom has five main elements to it:

- **Library.** This is perhaps the most important area as it is where metadata (tags) are added to images and where collections are created and organized (top image opposite)

- **Develop.** In this area color editing options can be applied to images (bottom image opposite)

- **Slideshow.** This acts like a filmstrip so that you can quickly see all of the images in a collection

- **Print.** This area enables you to prepare images for printing

- **Web.** This area enables you to prepare images for the Web

Aperture

Aperture is a workflow and image editing program for Mac users. Its main elements are:

- **Import.** Images can be imported directly from your camera into Aperture

- **Select and Edit.** This enables you to review your images, select the best ones and then edit them

- **Metadata.** Aperture has powerful tools for adding metadata and searching for images

Don't forget

Although workflow software may initially seem like an unnecessary step, it will save you an enormous amount of time the more that you work with digital images and build up a bigger library of shots.

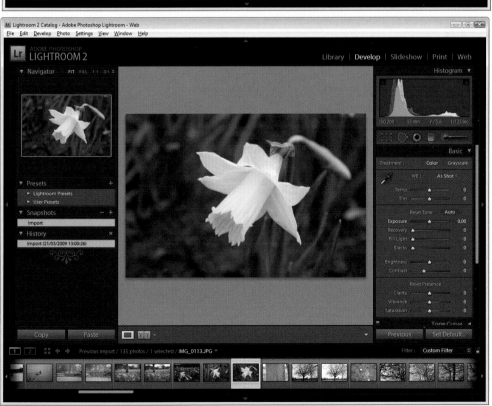

Metadata and Tags

Textual information can be attached to images to help identify them and make them searchable. This information is known as metadata and includes tags that are added to images. Some metadata is attached to an image when it is captured and other tags can be added during the workflow process.

Camera metadata

When an image is captured with a digital SLR a small file is created that contains information about the image. This is also known as EXIF data and includes information such as:

- Exposure

- Focal length

- Shutter speed

- Aperture

- Metering mode

- Make and model of camera

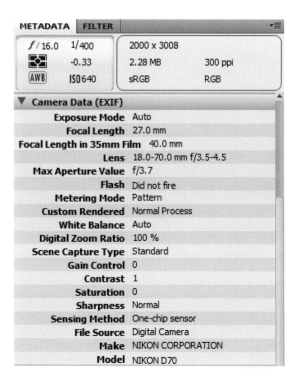

File metadata

In addition to camera metadata, images also have file metadata attached to them. This is a combination of information from when the image is captured on the camera and downloaded and edited on the computer. It includes information such as:

- File name

- File type

- File size

- Date created

- Date modified

- Dimensions in pixels

All of the metadata categories in the camera and file metadata can be used to search for images. For instance, you can search for an image according to a certain shutter speed or by the date created, or any combination of these categories.

▼ **File Properties**	
Filename	Paris_08 009.JPG
Document Type	JPEG file
Application	Ver.2.00
Date Created	13/07/2008, 11:10:54
Date File Modified	13/07/2008, 11:10:54
File Size	2.72 MB
Dimensions	3008 x 2000
Dimensions (in inches)	10.0" x 6.7"
Resolution	300 ppi
Bit Depth	8
Color Mode	RGB
Color Profile	sRGB IEC61966-2.1

Keywords

In addition to metadata that is added to images when they are captured, downloaded or edited it is also possible to add your own keywords. This is invaluable in terms of tagging them accurately so that they are easier to find (particularly if you have thousands of images to search through).

Categories

When adding your own keywords to images there are a number of straightforward categories under which you can group them, such as People, Places and Events. In programs such as Adobe Bridge, some categories are already created and you can then add keywords into these categories.

Hot tip

Create your own scheme for keywords and follow this consistently. This will make it easier when you are trying to search through thousands of images.

58

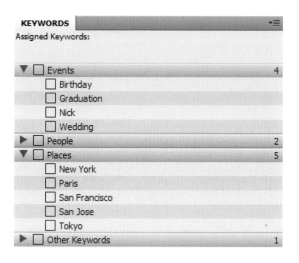

In all workflow programs it is possible to create your own categories, or sub-categories. This involves creating a category keyword, such as People for all images covering this subject, and then adding keywords within the category. Essentially, this is a method for managing your keywords so that they do not get out of control. Once categories and sub-categories have been created they can be used to search for images, as well as the individual keywords.

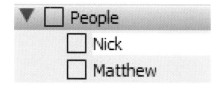

Adding keywords

The process for adding keywords is similar for all workflow software programs. Initially, an image, or images, is selected from an image library or collection, then keywords are selected from the appropriate list. This adds the keywords to the selected image.

Keyword Suggestions		▼
Flower	sacreur coer	Paris
canon_test...	Nick	Landscape
Light	Spring	

Keyword Set	Outdoor Photog... ⬍	▼
Landscape	Macro	Flowers & P...
Spring	Summer	Wildlife
Fall	Winter	People

Once keywords have been added to an image it usually has a visible tag denoting the presence of keywords. This can be clicked to display the attached keywords.

Photo has keywords

Searching for Images

The purpose of adding keywords to images is so that you can search for them and find them quickly. It is a good idea to get into the habit of adding keywords as soon as you start creating image libraries as it can be a frustrating business trying to find images if they have not been tagged.

Once you have added your own keywords to images they can be searched for over a variety of criteria.

Search box

Some workflow programs have a search box into which keywords can be typed to search for items:

All items with matching criteria are shown in the main window:

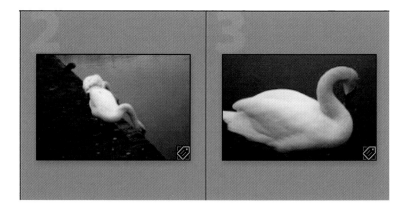

Each individual item can then be selected to perform other tasks such as image editing.

Categories

Another way to search for images is to use the categories of metadata. To do this, select a category from the filter function within the workflow software.

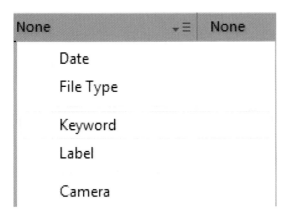

Once the category has been selected, click on an item to display all of the images with a certain attribute. (This can be a keyword, or another attribute such as the shutter speed of a certain image.)

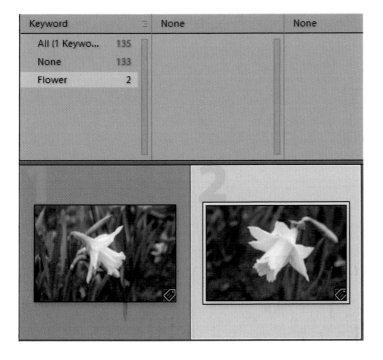

Image Editing Software

While this is not a book about image editing, there is one general point to be made about this: if you intend to undertake image editing to any serious degree then Adobe Photoshop is the undisputed leader in this field. This is not only a very powerful editing tool, it will also give you all of the functionality that you need for preparing images for print or for the Web.

Preparing for print

Photoshop has an extensive range of features for preparing images for printing, a lot of which are aimed at the professional printing process. However, for the home user there are a few basic rules to follow before you start printing your images:

- Calibrate your monitor. This will ensure that the colors on your monitor are as close as possible to the printed ones

- Use the highest resolution (i.e. physical size) images possible. This will ensure that they can be printed at high quality at a range of sizes. As a general rule, divide the number of pixels in your image (horizontally and vertically) by 300 to determine the size at which you can print the image. This is the number of pixels in an inch of a printed image that gives the best quality. So if you have an image that is 3000 x 2400 pixels then this could be printed at a size of 10 x 8 inches

- If you are printing images on your own printer, ensure that it is calibrated properly. This can be done with the printer driver that is installed with the printer and will allow for a variety of color settings and options. You can make this process as complicated as you want but it can come down to your own eye for looking at the final output

Preparing for the Web

While images that are going to be used for printing usually have to be of the highest resolution possible, images for use on the Web can be a lot smaller. This is because computer monitors are only able to display a limited number of pixels per inch on the screen, so large images appear at a much bigger size (and also take longer to download). In Photoshop there is a Save for Web function which allows you to optimize images for use on the Web. Through this you can select the file format, physical size and quality of the image that you are going to use on the Web.

Hot tip

Computer monitors can be calibrated by using the Adobe Gamma program.

Don't forget

Very high quality prints can be achieved from online print services and also photographic retailers and stores.

RAW Images

In many respects the RAW image format has transformed the way that a lot of photographers operate. Although some compact digital cameras now have this option, it is something that originated with digital SLR cameras. The RAW format is unprocessed, uncompressed data that enables you to perform a lot of the processes that are done automatically when file formats such as JPEG are created. Image data for RAW images is held in a separate file which is used to make the corrections to the RAW file. In many ways the RAW file format is the equivalent of working with a 35mm negative.

RAW images can be processed using the image editor related to the manufacturer of your digital SLR. (This will usually be provided on a CD that comes with the camera, or it can be downloaded from the manufacturer's website.) Alternatively Photoshop can be used. In this case you will need a Camera RAW plug-in which will enable you to process RAW files.

When working with RAW files there are a number of elements which you can edit manually:

- White balance
- Exposure
- Brightness and contrast
- Vibrance and saturation
- Color adjustment
- Sharpening
- Noise reduction

These elements can also be edited once the RAW file has been saved in another format but you usually get more control when you work with the RAW file.

Once you have finished editing the RAW file you can then save it as a JPEG or a TIFF which will enable you to use it for printing or on the Web.

Even if you do not use RAW regularly in your workflow it is worth trying it out to see if it gives you more flexibility.

Workflow Checklist

Everyone will organize their own digital workflow slightly differently but these are some of the general functions that should be included:

- Create an image folder structure on your computer

- Download images from your camera

- Assign each set of downloaded images to a specific folder

- If required, split downloaded images into new folders (for instance, you may have images of different subject matter on your memory card)

- Check your images for any obvious mistakes. Discard any unsuitable images

- Use a workflow software program to help manage and organize your images

- Assign keywords to your images

- Perform a test search to ensure that you have assigned the keywords correctly

- Perform image editing tasks (do this on copies of the originals, not the originals themselves)

- Calibrate your monitor to ensure a consistent color display for images on screen and when they are printed

- For printing, use the largest images you can and divide the number of pixels by 300 to work out the optimum print size

- Print a draft of your images for proofing purposes. If necessary, perform additional editing to correct any inconsistencies in the images

- Optimize images for the Web to ensure they are suitable in terms of physical size and file size. In general, the JPEG file format should be used for images on the Web

- Back up your images (do this when you first download them and then periodically during the workflow process)

Don't forget

Once you have downloaded your images from your memory card delete them from the card. This will prevent the build-up of hundreds of images on the card.

4 Camera Techniques

This chapter offers some straightforward techniques that can be used to turn basic holiday snaps into quality photos.

Camera Orientation

Digital SLR cameras can help produce high quality images. However, in a lot of cases a good eye for a photograph can be just as important as the equipment being used. Part of this involves changing the angle at which an image is being viewed. There are a number of ways in which this can be achieved, but the simplest is to change the camera's orientation. This is a case of rotating the camera by 90 degrees so that the image is captured in portrait rather than landscape.

A good eye for a photograph can be more important than the equipment being used

Even if you have taken one good photograph, this simple technique of changing the orientation can ensure that you have another impressive shot, which shows the subject from a different perspective. Since you are not using up any film it is always worthwhile to take shots with different orientations so that you can compare them at a later date. Also, if you want to crop the image you will have more scope to do this if you have the main subject in different orientations.

With the examples on the facing page the top image is captured in portrait orientation, but the feeling of the scene is changed considerably simply by changing the orientation of the camera so that the bottom image is in landscape.

Tilting

Another option for changing the orientation is rotating the camera to an angle rather than holding it horizontal or vertical. This can be particularly effective with landscape shots to emphasize angles. However, it is an effect that should be used as an extra option once more conventional shots have been taken.

Cropping and Image Size

The physical size of an image is an important factor in assessing the quality and size of printed images. For images straight out of the camera this is a fairly simple calculation: the pixel dimensions of the image divided by 300 (the optimum setting for printing images). However, if you want to edit images then this may have an impact on the pixel dimensions. This is particularly true if the image is going to be cropped, one of the most popular image editing techniques and one that can be done with image editing software or within photo kiosks at photography printing outlets.

Cropping involves removing unwanted areas from an image. This is usually done by selecting the area you want to keep (as a rectangle within the image) and then discarding the rest of the image. See the two examples on the facing page. Obviously, this has an impact on the pixel dimensions of the image as some of the original pixels have been discarded.

If you are cropping an image it is important to make sure that the edited image is still large enough to be printed at a good quality at the required size. To check this, divide the pixel dimensions of the cropped image by 300. So, for example, if you want to print at 7 inches by 5 inches then the edited image will need to be approximately 2100 pixels by 1500 pixels, or more.

The issue of cropping and image size is one of the reasons why it is always valuable to capture images at the maximum resolution; you do not always know how much you will want to keep or remove in an image but with the highest resolution available you will have a lot more flexibility if you want to edit your images.

Don't forget

The resolution of images when they are printed can be greater than 300 pixels per inch, but try not to let it fall too far below this number.

Frame Filling

In some instances it is advisable to fill the frame with as much of the subject as possible. However, if you think you will want to crop an image it is better to leave some extra room around the subject when the image is captured. Then, as long as the resolution is large enough, the final image can be cropped and printed to a high enough quality.

Using Bracketing

One of the problems with film photography is that you never really know how an image is going to look until it is printed. With digital cameras this drawback is largely removed by the facility to review images with the LCD panel as soon as they have been taken. However, LCD panels do not always give a totally accurate depiction of the color and exposure of an image and it can sometimes be difficult to see the image clearly, particularly if there is sun or direct light shining on the LCD. In order to make sure you capture a perfectly exposed shot, the technique of bracketing can be used.

Bracketing is a photographic technique that involves capturing an image for a range of exposure settings. This means that at least one of the shots should be correctly exposed. To use bracketing, a camera has to have an option for exposure compensation but since almost all digital SLRs have this they are ideal for bracketing.

Don't forget

For more information about exposure compensation see Chapter Six.

Don't forget

Most digital SLR cameras have an auto bracketing function. When this is selected the camera will take three shots using different exposure values. This is usually done by pressing the shutter release button three separate times and the exposure is altered for each shot.

To use bracketing, capture an image in any shooting mode, e.g. automatic, aperture priority, shutter speed priority or fully manual. Then select an exposure compensation value to make the image either darker or lighter. To make an image lighter select a positive exposure compensation value and to make it darker use a negative value. For bracketing, use at least one example above and one below the settings for the initial shot. Remember, images sometimes look slightly different on a computer as opposed to the camera's LCD panel.

> Bracketing ensures that an image is captured for a range of exposure settings

Better Safe

Bracketing is especially important for locations that you may not be visiting again. The middle image on the facing page is correctly exposed, but two more were captured using +/−1 exposure compensation, in case these images were an improvement.

70

Capturing Macro Shots

Macro photography is another term for close-up shots. These types of shot take advantage of a camera's ability to capture images at very close distances. Digital SLRs can be fitted with a variety of macro lenses to achieve close-up shots and it is certainly worth thinking about one for your lens collection.

One of the main issues with macro shots is focusing. This is because the focusing has to be very accurate at such a close distance as there is little margin for error. One problem is that the object has to be very still for the auto-focus to work, so if there is even slight movement this will be magnified greatly as far as the focusing is concerned. So if you are taking photos of subjects such as flowers or insects, try and do so when there is very little wind, or use some form of wind break to ensure that the subject is as still as possible.

Macro shots can also cause problems with focusing if there is not enough contrast within the shot – since you will be focusing on one small area of an object there may not be enough contrast within that area. If this is the case try finding an edge within the subject (this may involve moving the camera, focusing and then recomposing the shot while still keeping the shutter release button held down to retain focus) but make sure it is at the same distance as the intended subject. Another option is to use a black and white striped card and hold this at the point of focus within the image.

Another issue is that close-up shots have a very narrow depth of field, i.e. very little of the object is in focus. This means that you have to focus very accurately to make sure the correct part of the image is in focus. In the image on the facing page the center of the shot is in focus, while the background is blurred due to the very small depth of field.

Backgrounds

Be careful with backgrounds in macro shots to ensure they do not detract from the main subject. One way to do this is to have a wide aperture (e.g. f2.8, f4 or f5) so that the depth of field is very small, and the background becomes blurred so as not to be a distraction.

Zooming Effectively

For a digital SLR camera with a zoom lens, it is always worthwhile to experiment with the zoom function for particular shots. In some cases the wide angle shot may be more effective, while in others the zoomed version will be better. In an ideal situation, both versions of the image will be effective.

When working with zoom it is important to use it creatively, not just presume that a zoomed version of a wide angle shot will work well. In some cases it will, while in others it may take a little more work to get the best picture.

When using zoom, the first option is to capture the same shot at different focal lengths, i.e. with varying amounts of zoom applied. Start with the zoom at its widest angle, i.e. fully retracted, and then retake the picture as you zoom in closer and closer. This should provide a good range of shots of the same image, but some will be more effective than others.

Another way to use the zoom is to take a wide angled shot and then focus on a particular aspect of a subject with the zoom. This could mean that you take the

Take the zoomed shot from a different viewpoint

zoomed shot from a different viewpoint, as with the two images on the facing page. The top image is a standard wide angle shot of the subject. A closer version could have also been taken with the zoom from the same position, but instead the angle of shooting was changed so that the zoomed image is of another part of the main subject. Taken together, the two images manage to convey both the structure and the character of the church.

Watch the Border

When capturing shots at the highest zoom setting it is worthwhile leaving a small border between the subject and the outside of the image. This will allow for the image to be cropped slightly during the printing process if necessary.

Keeping the Camera Steady

For certain types of shots it is vital to keep the camera as steady as possible. This is because if the shutter speed falls below about 1/60th second then the camera will move slightly as the shot is being captured. This can result in a slightly blurred image caused by what is known as "camera shake".

The best way to keep the camera steady and avoid camera shake is to use a tripod. These come in a variety of sizes and weights but even a small, lightweight one will greatly assist in keeping the

Get into the habit of taking a tripod with you whenever you are using your camera

camera still while the shot is being taken. Get into the habit of taking a tripod with you whenever you are using your camera as you never know when you might need to take a shot with a slow shutter speed.

Steady as it Goes

Conditions that will require extra support include: night shots; indoor shots; slow shutter speeds to create a blurred effect for motion, and a camera with a large telephoto lens.

In some cases, even the pressing of the shutter release button when a camera is on a tripod can cause slight camera shake. To remove the risk of this, the self-timer option can be used so that the camera fires automatically after a certain period of time once the timer has been activated. Alternatively, some cameras have cable releases or infrared remote controls that can be used to take the shot.

If you do not have a tripod a good alternative is to rest the camera on a cushion. It is worthwhile carrying a small cushion, or bean-bag, around with you when you are taking pictures so that you can always have a steady platform for your camera. If all else fails, try supporting your camera against a bench or a door-frame.

5 Lighting Issues

Lighting is crucial in photography. This chapter discusses various lighting issues and shows how you can use light to create stunning results.

White Balance

Since cameras are not as clever as the human eye, they sometimes have trouble distinguishing between different types of light. This is because different light sources have what is known as different "color temperatures". This means that the color reflected from an object is different depending on the type of source light. For instance, the color reflected from a piece of white paper in direct sunlight will be different from that reflected from a piece of white paper under fluorescent lighting. Since the human eye is so sophisticated, it can compensate for these changes so that the original object always looks the same – the piece of paper always looks white. However, cameras cannot do this so they have to compensate with a function known as white balance to try and ensure that objects always appear the correct color, regardless of the light source.

Digital cameras have a default setting for measuring the white balance in an image. This works by assessing the type of light in the image and then adjusting the white balance accordingly. However, this does not always work perfectly – particularly under artificial lighting – so manual adjustments can be made for different lighting conditions. These take into account different external and internal lighting conditions and usually cover: auto, shade, sunlight, cloudy, fluorescent, incandescent and flash. Adjusting the white balance settings is particularly useful in artificial lighting conditions and is worth experimenting with.

In most cases it is also possible to preset the white balance for certain shooting conditions. This involves selecting the appropriate white balance option from the camera's white balance menu. Once this has been done, place a piece of white or gray card at the point where you are going to capture the image. From the white balance menu select the option for manually recording the white balance and capture the image with the card in the center. The camera will then calculate the required white balance for these lighting conditions and adjust the lighting in the final image accordingly.

In the examples on the opposite page the top image was captured using an incorrect white balance setting (cloudy) resulting in an unnatural color cast in the image, while the one on the bottom used a correct setting (fluorescent). If in doubt about the lighting in a particular scene, capture it at several different white balance settings to ensure that at least one image will be correct.

Beware

When reviewing the white balance in an image on a camera's LCD panel it is not always possible to get an accurate impression of the effect due to the size of the screen. The only way to be completely sure is to view the image on a computer.

78

Don't forget

If you preset the white balance, make sure you set it to another mode (such as Auto) before you take a shot in different lighting conditions.

Indoor Shots

Light is one of the essential ingredients for any photograph but this does not mean that you have to have bright sunlight to capture a good image. Indeed, with a bit of planning and experience it is possible to take good pictures in any lighting conditions.

One area about which people are sometimes unsure is taking pictures indoors. In a lot of cases this will result in the photographer immediately activating the flash on the camera. Sometimes this will work, but only if the subject is within range of the flash. However, for a large indoor area, such as the interior of a church, the flash will be ineffective; it will light up a small area in the foreground while the rest of the image will look too dark. Instead of using the flash a more versatile implement for indoor photography is a tripod. This will enable you to use a slow shutter speed on the camera, thus allowing enough light to enter the camera to capture a well-lit scene without the need for flash.

When capturing images indoors without the flash the use of a tripod is essential to keep the camera still for a slow shutter speed. If the camera were to be hand-held then the image would end up looking blurred due to camera shake. Make sure you have a sturdy tripod and pay particular attention to the tripod head on which the camera is mounted. This should be as steady as possible. Once the tripod is set up, set the camera to aperture priority mode and select an aperture for the type of shot you want to capture (a wide aperture for a small area in focus and a narrow aperture for a large area in focus). The camera will then select a suitable shutter speed, which may be well over a second. If possible, use the camera's self-timer or a shutter release cable to trip the shutter release as this will reduce further the chance of camera shake.

The top image on the facing page was taken with a wide aperture (f4.2) and a shutter speed of 1/8th second. Due to the amount of light from the candles this was enough to illuminate the scene and give it a very evocative feel. In the bottom image on the facing page a high ISO value of 1600 was used to increase the camera's sensitivity to light. This meant that a faster shutter speed of 1/60th second could be used and so the camera could still be hand-held rather than put on a tripod.

Hot tip

Check your camera's manual to see the available range of ISO settings. This can have a significant impact on capturing indoor shots as a higher ISO range may enable you to capture shots without the need for a tripod.

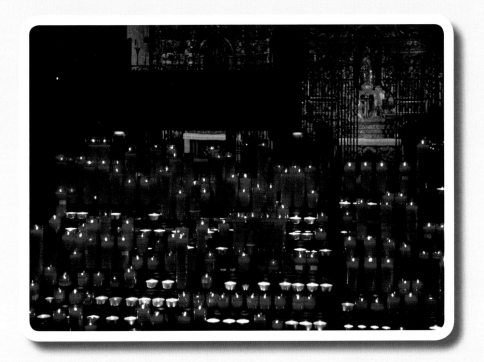

Fill-in Flash

Although front lighting is a common option for a variety of photographic situations (see page 86) it can have its disadvantages too. One of these is seen when capturing images of people. If the main subjects are lit from the front they may appear bright but the light inevitably causes them to squint, or shade their faces from the bright sunlight. This usually results in a very unnatural and strained-looking portrait.

One solution to this problem is to position the subjects with the sun behind them. This removes the strain on their eyes and allows them to look more relaxed. However, this causes its own problems as the back lighting results in their faces being in shadow. This is the case in the top image on the facing page, where the subjects look unnaturally shaded even though it is a bright, sunny day.

Don't forget

Fill-in flash can be used for any backlit subject, not just a portrait.

82

This is the best way to ensure a well-balanced portrait when a subject is backlit by the sun

The solution to this problem lies in a technique known as fill-in flash. It may seem strange to use the flash when you are outside in the sun but this is the best way to ensure a well-balanced portrait when a subject is backlit by the sun. To achieve this, you have to actively turn on the flash to fire on every shot (if the camera is in automatic mode it will calculate that there is enough light in the scene without the need for flash). Once the flash has been activated it is just a case of taking the shot as normal. This is how the bottom image on the facing page was captured; the flash lights up the faces and this balances out the scene with the sunlit background. In some cases you may need to experiment with the distance between you and your subjects so that you get the correct amount of flash falling on their faces. Consult your camera's manual to see the range of your flash.

Another way to capture this type of image is to use a light source to the side of the subjects. This can produce the most sympathetic lighting effect and means that fill-in flash is not required.

Polarizing Filters

The use of image editing programs means that a lot of special effects that were previously created using filters on cameras can now be done on computers. However, there is still a use for filters in some creative situations and there is one filter that should always be considered. This is a polarizing filter (or polarizer) and this is a filter that works in a way that cannot be re-created on a computer.

Polarizing filters can be attached to the front of lenses on digital SLR cameras. On a digital SLR camera the effect is visible as you turn the outer ring of the filter.

A polarizing filter operates by physically reducing the amount of glare in a scene created by vertical light. This allows for more prominence to be given to horizontal light in a scene.

Polarizing filters are also excellent for reducing glare from water and glass

Polarizing filters are also excellent for reducing glare from water and glass because of the way they block out light from certain angles. To do this, it is best to stand at an angle to the scene you are capturing (approximately 35 degrees) and then rotate the front ring on the polarizing filter until you see the glare start to disappear or reduce.

Polarizing filters can also be used to improve the saturation and color of landscape shots, since they remove some of the unwanted vertical light in the scene. To do this, you have to be at approximately 90 degrees to the sun. It is therefore a useful option for capturing shots in the otherwise harsh midday sun. Since the sun is overhead, it is naturally at 90 degrees and you can use the polarizing filter to try and remove the harsh midday glare. The top image on the facing page was taken without a filter and the glare from the sun is visible across the image; the sky is also burnt out. In the bottom image a polarizing filter has been used, which has cut out the glare from the sun and also greatly improved the color and saturation of the sky.

Don't forget

Polarizing filters are not cheap but they are a good investment if you are going to be taking a lot of landscape shots.

84

Beware

Polarizing filters do not usually cut out all of the glare from glass or water, but they can reduce it greatly.

Types of Natural Light

Since lighting is so important to photography, it is only natural that there is terminology for more than one type of light. These cover both daytime and night shooting, but in normal daytime conditions the main three types of light that interest the photographer are backlight, frontlight and sidelight.

Backlight occurs when the main source of light is behind a subject. This can cause problems for exposure (since the subject is in shadow while the background is brightly lit) but it also offers more creative opportunities. Once you learn how to set exposures for different parts of a scene you can use backlighting to create silhouettes or expose the main subject for an artistic effect. This can be particularly striking for macro (close-up) photography where the main subject is very small and is illuminated from behind.

Frontlight is the opposite to backlight and occurs when the main source of light is behind the photographer and facing the subject. This creates a more even exposure but you have to be careful about the time of day when capturing frontlit subjects outside. If it is too near midday the sun will be too high in the sky. This will result in images that appear too harsh and with too much contrast; the sun at this time is at its brightest but this gives a "flat" light in photographic terms. In terms of lighting conditions for consistently good images, frontlight is the best bet. The two images on the facing page show the difference between a standard frontlit and backlit image. The top image is backlit i.e. the sun is behind the main subject, leaving it in shade. The bottom image is frontlit, giving it a much better overall appearance since it is illuminated directly by the main light source.

The other main type of lighting is sidelight. This is where the main light source is at the side of the subject. This is a particularly effective lighting source for portraits since it provides a good contrast on the subject's face: one side is brightly lit while the other is in shade. However, it is important to get the balance right or else the contrast between the two will be too great.

Experiment

Capture the same subject at different times and in different lighting conditions, to see the effects this has on the image.

The Golden Hour

Great photography is not just about the direction and amount of light in an image. It is also about the quality of light. This is because light has differing qualities throughout the day, particularly sunlight: at midday the sun is at its strongest and, curiously, this is the worst time to capture images. Midday sun is too harsh and powerful and although it will produce a well-lit image the quality of the color will be lacking in depth and saturation. For the best photographs, the ideal lighting conditions usually occur approximately one hour after sunrise and one hour before sunset. This is known as the Golden Hour.

The reason that the Golden Hour is so good for photography is because of the angle at which the light hits its subjects and because at these times it produces a deep glow rather than the harsh glare of midday sun. The morning and the evening Golden Hours produce slightly different effects: the morning sun has a soft golden effect while the evening sun tends to have a stronger orange glow with a bit more depth to it. Once you have experienced capturing images in the Golden Hour you will realize why it is so treasured by photographers.

Although the Golden Hour can produce stunning photographic results it usually takes a bit more effort on the part of the photographer. In the morning you will have to be up and away before sunrise and in the evening you may not finish shooting until well into the evening. The essential thing is to make the most of these lighting opportunities when they present themselves. This may mean checking out a few shooting locations during normal daylight hours so you know exactly where to go when the Golden Hour occurs. You do not want to be wasting time finding locations when the light is at its best. A bit of forward planning can make all the difference when dealing with the Golden Hour.

The other thing to be aware of about the Golden Hour is that it is short. This means that you will not have a lot of time to move from location to location. It is best to pick a subject that you want to capture and then concentrate on a few top quality shots.

A final point about the Golden Hour is that it can produce great results in two directions. For instance, you may be looking at a fantastic sunset but if you turn around you may see a subject bathed in a glorious golden, orange light.

Hot tip

Make the effort to utilize the Golden Hour in your photography wherever you are. You will see a marked improvement in your images.

Creating Grainy Effects

The aperture and shutter speed help determine the amount of light that can enter the camera for a particular shot. In addition to this, there is another function that can affect how light enters the camera. This is known as the ISO setting, or film speed in standard film photography terminology. A standard film speed is 100 or 200 for brightly lit conditions. Digital SLR cameras have ISO equivalent ratings, usually in the range of 100–1600 (or greater in some cases).

ISO speed refers to how quickly light is captured by the image sensor for a particular shot. If the ISO equivalent rating is 100 or 200 it means that the image sensor is less sensitive to light and so can capture images in bright conditions. However, a higher ISO rating means that the image sensor is more sensitive to light and so can capture images in more dimly lit conditions. Higher ISO ratings can be used for indoor shots or night shots.

ISO speed refers to how quickly light is captured by the image sensor for a particular shot

In general, leave your camera on the default ISO equivalent rating which will probably be 100 or 200. This will deal with most normal daylight situations but remember that ISO ratings can be changed from shot to shot on a digital camera.

One option for ISO ratings is to create deliberately grainy effects in images. This is done by using a high ISO rating, such as 800 or 1600, which can create "noise" in an image. Noise is the speckled effect that is created by randomly distributed pixels within an image. With a high ISO setting the amount of noise increases and if it is created deliberately it is generally done for artistic purposes.

More digital SLR cameras tend to create less noise than compact ones, even in low level lighting conditions. If this is the case, grainy effects can be created with image editing software.

6 Exposure and Metering

Understanding exposure and metering gives you confidence when taking photos and opens up a number of creative techniques, such as depth of field.

Depth of Field

Depth of field refers to the area within an image (from front to back) that is in focus. A large depth of field means that a large area of the image is in focus, while a small depth of field means that only a small area of the image is in focus. The depth of field for a particular image is determined by the focal length of the lens being used, the distance between the photographer, the main subject and the background, and, most importantly, the aperture being used.

The choice of depth of field to deploy will depend on the type of image you want to capture and this is where a bit of thought needs to go into the creative process: do you want an image with foreground, main subject and background in focus, or do you want to isolate the main subject with a blurred background? In general, landscape shots use a large depth of field (narrow aperture – large f-number) to keep everything in focus and single subject shots (such as portraits) benefit from a smaller depth of field (wide aperture – small f-number), thus causing the background to be blurred and giving more emphasis to the main subject.

The best way to take control over depth of field is to set your camera to aperture priority. This means that you can select the aperture and the camera will then automatically select a suitable shutter speed to expose the image correctly. Remember, a wide aperture will result in a faster shutter speed and vice versa. Also, the smaller the f-number, the wider the aperture, e.g. on some lenses f2.8 is the widest aperture while f22 is the narrowest. So to try and isolate a single image, select a wide aperture (f2.8, f4 or f5.6) and for a scene where you want as large an area as possible in focus, select a narrow aperture (f16 or f22). For an image where depth of field is not important select a mid-range aperture (f8 or f11) to give the best color saturation in the image. The image on the facing page was captured with an aperture of f16 to create a large depth of field to ensure that as much of the image was in focus as possible.

> The best way to take control over depth of field is to set your camera to aperture priority

Don't forget

Once you have mastered depth of field you will be able to start taking much more control over the technical side of your photography and also the composition of scenes.

Blurring the Background

One of the main uses for depth of field is to create a blurred background. The amount of blurring can be altered by changing the camera's aperture and this can be used to create differing effects. Each effect can produce a worthwhile image and it is up to you to decide the type of effect that you want to achieve.

To create a blurred background, the camera has to be set on aperture priority mode so that you can manually select the aperture and the camera will then automatically set a suitable shutter speed. Start with a reasonably narrow aperture such as f11. This should render the background slightly blurry, as with the top image on the facing page. One way to try and create a narrow depth of field is to get as close in to the subject as possible and leave as large a distance as you can between the main subject and the background. Also, by using a zoom lens and zooming in on the main subject, a narrower depth of field will be created (i.e. less of the image will be in focus).

Once you have captured one image, widen the aperture on the camera, i.e. set it to a lower f-number. Take another image with an aperture of approximately f8 to see the difference between this image and the first one. The middle image on the facing page was captured with this setting, resulting in a greater degree of blurring in the background. For the final image, set the aperture to its widest setting, usually f4 or f5.6, and capture the image again. This will create an image with the greatest degree of blurring, as with the bottom image on the facing page.

Beware

If the background in an image is too cluttered it may detract from the main subject.

Don't forget

Some digital SLR cameras have a depth of field preview option that enables you to see the amount of an image that is going to be in focus at a particular aperture setting.

Uses

Some subjects that benefit from softening the background include children, flowers, insects and close-up objects that can be isolated with the background a reasonable distance behind.

Software Option

Backgrounds can also be removed with image editing software by selecting the background and then adding various blur effects from the filters menu.

Matrix Metering

Measuring the amount of light in a scene is known as metering. Most cameras offer different options for the way this is done. Digital SLRs have three or four metering options, with the default one usually being the matrix method. This works by looking at areas within the whole scene and calculating the amount of light accordingly. This is done by comparing the image with a database compiled from thousands of images taken in a vast range of lighting conditions. The matrix method compares the current scene with those in the database and when it finds a similarly lit scene it applies the required shutter speed and aperture settings. The matrix method can be used successfully for the majority of photographic situations but it is not foolproof and can become confused by complex lighting conditions.

Don't forget

If you are unsure about light metering, leave the camera on matrix metering as this will work well in the majority of shooting situations.

If light is spread evenly throughout an image then the matrix metering method should work well. However, if there are large dark and light areas within an image then this could cause problems for the matrix method and either sport metering or center-weighted metering should be used.

In general, matrix metering can be used in most lighting conditions. The top image on the facing page looks as though it could cause problems for the matrix metering method, since the building is a lot lighter than the dark background. However, since there are reasonably equal areas of both light and dark in the image the matrix method can assimilate this and adjust the exposure accordingly. If either of the light or dark areas were significantly larger than the other then this could cause problems for the matrix method.

In general, matrix metering can be used in most lighting conditions

In the bottom image on the facing page the light and shade could potentially cause problems for the matrix method. However, since this is evenly distributed throughout the image the matrix method can easily find an equivalent image in its database and so expose the image correctly.

96

Spot Metering

Spot metering is a method of measuring light in a scene; it is less frequently used than matrix metering. However, although it is not such a common method it is still very important for specific types of lighting conditions.

Spot metering usually has to be specifically selected from within the camera's menu system (or sometimes from a dial on the camera body) and it works by taking a light reading from a very small area in the center of the viewfinder. The exposure for the scene is then set for this reading, regardless of the amount of light in the rest of the scene. For some scenes, this does not produce accurate results since the amount of light in the center may be different from that in other parts of the scene (matrix metering would be able to take this into account and expose the image correctly).

Spot metering works by taking a light reading from a very small area in the center of the viewfinder

The time to use spot metering is when it is important to expose one particular element of a scene correctly. This could be a very dark subject on a light background, or vice versa. However, the point where the spot metering reading is taken does not have to be in the center of the required scene. If necessary, a spot metering reading can be taken from anywhere in the scene and, using exposure lock, the scene can be recomposed and captured with the spot metering reading being retained.

In the bottom image on the facing page a spot meter reading was taken from the scene through the window, resulting in it being exposed correctly. However, since there was not enough light for the surrounding frame this is under-exposed, i.e. too dark. In order to get the frame exposed correctly, a spot metering reading was taken by pointing the camera at the frame, locking the exposure, and recomposing and capturing the scene. However, this causes the scene behind it to be over-exposed, i.e. too light, since more light was needed to expose the frame.

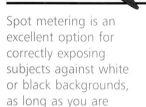

More Spot Metering

As shown on the previous page, spot metering can be used to correctly expose certain areas within a scene. Depending on the area that is spot metered, this can result in the rest of the image being either over- or under-exposed. However, this does not mean that spot metering cannot be used to try and get the whole of a scene exposed correctly.

One situation where spot metering can be used is when there are large areas of dark and light within a scene; conditions which could confuse a matrix meter reading. In cases like this a spot meter reading can be taken from a midtone area within the scene. A midtone is an area between the darkest and lightest areas within the image. If a spot metering is taken from here then there is more chance that the rest of the image will be correctly exposed too.

A midtone is an area between the darkest and lightest areas within the image

If a spot metering is being taken from an area that is off-center in the viewfinder then exposure lock will have to be used (unless the shot is being captured in fully manual mode, in which case the spot meter reading can be taken from the midtone area, and then the exposure settings can be applied before the scene is recomposed for shooting).

Spot metering can also be used to correctly expose single subjects against a particular background. In the top image on the facing page a matrix meter reading was taken initially, resulting in the main subject being under-exposed since the exposure was set for the larger area of water.

In the bottom image, a spot meter reading was taken from the fisherman before the image was recomposed for capturing the shot. The result is that the correct exposure has been achieved for the main subject since the meter reading was taken directly from this point. Since the fisherman is darker than the background, the water is now slightly over-exposed, but this serves to create a better contrast between the subject and the background, which results in a much more satisfactory image.

Don't forget

In photographic terms the darkest areas of an image are known as the shadows and the lightest areas are known as the highlights.

Exposure Compensation

For some lighting conditions even digital SLRs can find it difficult to meter a scene correctly, such as when there are very dark and very light areas within the same scene. Sometimes this can be adjusted by using a different method of metering from the default one. Another way of adjusting the exposure in a scene is to use exposure compensation.

Exposure compensation is regulated by the Exposure Value (EV) control on a camera. This is usually a button on the body of the digital SLR. What the EV control does is allow more, or less, light into the camera for a particular exposure setting. This is usually measured in one step increments and each step up or down the scale is the equivalent of one exposure stop. For instance, if a +1 EV value is applied this is the same as reducing the shutter speed by one step or increasing the aperture by one step. The majority of digital cameras can go to a minimum of +/-2 on the EV scale and some go as far as +/-5.

The reason that the EV control is important is because you can use it to physically change the amount of light entering the camera above or below the metering reading. In either aperture priority or shutter speed priority, the same amount of light will still enter the camera regardless of how you change one or other of the values. The EV control enables you to keep a particular aperture or shutter speed setting and then adjust the amount of light accordingly. This is useful if you need a certain aperture for depth of field or a shutter speed for freezing motion.

To make an image lighter, i.e. increase the exposure, use a positive EV value, and to make an image darker, i.e. decrease the exposure, use a negative EV value. In the top image on the facing page the aperture was set to f16 to achieve a reasonable depth of field in the image. However, the camera's metering system exposed the image for the pillars, leaving the background over-exposed. With the same aperture and shutter speed settings the EV value was set to -2 to try and decrease the exposure in the image, i.e. allow less light into the camera. The result is that the background is correctly exposed and although the pillars are now slightly under-exposed they have retained enough detail to create an effective overall image. If you experiment with the EV controls you will be able to capture well-exposed images in a variety of lighting conditions, without having to change any other settings.

Creating Silhouettes

Silhouettes can be one of the most evocative and dramatic forms of photograph. They can be created from landscapes, buildings and people. In fact, almost any object can be turned into a silhouette in the correct lighting conditions.

The secret to creating a silhouette is in having a subject against a bright, backlit background. This will ensure that there is more light falling behind the subject than on the front of it. In a normal photograph this would probably produce a shaded subject that was still visible but not silhouetted. To turn the shaded subject into a silhouette it is usually necessary to take a metering reading from the backlit background. This will require locking the exposure on the background. Once the exposure has been locked on the background, the shot can then be recomposed to include the foreground subject that will be rendered as the silhouette once the shot is taken. This happens because the exposure is set for the light background, i.e. there will be a reasonably fast shutter speed and a narrow aperture setting. This will allow enough light to enter the camera to expose the background correctly but there will not be enough for the foreground subject. This will result in the main subject being under-exposed, i.e. dark. Since the background is a lot lighter than the subject the under-exposure should be enough to create a black silhouette effect. If not, try locking the exposure on an even lighter area.

> The secret to creating a silhouette is having a subject against a bright, backlit background

The image on the facing page was taken in the evening when the sun was setting. The exposure was locked on the orange glow in the sky, which provided a setting that was suitable to capture the sky and create the silhouette. The colors of the setting sun give an extra dimension to the silhouette and this is always worth bearing in mind when capturing this type of shot. Sometimes it is worthwhile taking another shot, with the exposure locked on a slightly darker area of the background, so that there is more definition visible in the main subject.

Hot tip

Silhouettes of people can be captured using the technique described on this page. This adds an extra dimension to portraits and is a very effective option.

Dynamic Range

The way the lightest and darkest areas within an image are depicted is known as the dynamic range of the image. Ideally, both extremes of the scale should still retain enough detail to be clearly identified. However, it is a known problem of most digital cameras that they are not ideal at always accurately capturing the full dynamic range in an image. This means that in some images the light areas will be too light (i.e. burned out) or the dark areas will be too dark.

To test the dynamic range of your own camera, find a location with one very dark and one very light area. Take two identical images, one with the exposure locked on the darkest area and one with the exposure locked on the lightest area. This creates images like those below, neither of which is ideal.

One way around the problem of dynamic range is to take the same image at different exposure settings and hope that one of them is acceptable. Another possible solution is to take a spot metering reading from a midtone area within the image and use this to capture the scene. Luckily, dynamic range problems only occur in a small proportion of shooting conditions, but it is worth being aware of them so that you can make adjustments if required.

Hot tip

Photoshop can be used to create HDR (High Dynamic Range) images. This is where several images with different exposures are combined to give a composite image. This contains an accurate exposure across the whole dynamic range and can create some stunning images.

7 People and Portraits

Photos of people are universally popular and can be used for a variety of purposes. This chapter details methods for capturing both groups of people and individuals.

Distances and Angles

For every image of people there are several variations that can be used to create markedly different results. This can be done by changing the distance from which the image is captured and also the angle.

The distance between the photographer and the subject can have a significant impact on the perception of anyone looking at the images. If an image is captured from a greater distance then the emphasis on the people will be reduced since the whole scene will have greater prominence. As you get closer to the subject for the shot the emphasis shifts from the background to the subject itself. Changing the shooting distance can be done by using a zoom lens or you can physically move closer. Of the two, using the zoom is probably better as you will not then be crowding the subject.

> The distance between the photographer and the subject can have a significant impact on the images

The top image on the facing page shows a subject taken from a distance, while the bottom one is a medium range shot and the middle one is a close-up. This results in the bottom image having a much greater impact. Which type you choose depends on what you want to convey. If you want to show people in context then shooting from further away is better.

As well as changing the shooting distance it can also be beneficial to change the angle of shooting. This can create a very different impression for the same subject. For instance, a shot from below can create an imposing impression while one from the side is more relaxed. Similarly, a shot taken from above creates an image with a greater sense of space, as if the subject were looking up into the sky.

Beware

If you are too far away from the subject they will get lost in the background and the image will lose a lot of its impact and significance.

Getting Low

Sometimes it pays to lie down on the ground and capture an image from this angle as it creates a better perspective.

Group Shots

Everyone likes looking at images of other people, whether they be family snapshots or group shots in the workplace. However, not everyone enjoys having their picture taken and this can cause problems for the photographer. The issue is exacerbated when groups of people are involved; not only do you have to try and ensure that everyone is looking enthusiastic about posing for a photo but you also have to try and compose and capture the image so that everyone is positioned correctly.

One of the crucial issues when creating group photographs is timing. Initially it is important to give people enough time before you plan to capture the image. People usually like to prepare themselves before having their photo taken so let them know what you are planning to do. It is also important to give yourself enough time, both before you take the shot and while you are doing it. The more time you have for composing and capturing

Give people enough time before you plan to capture the image

the shot, the more time there will be to get everyone relaxed and enjoying the experience.

As far as the composition of group shots is concerned, it is not ideal to have a straight line of people (see top image on the facing page). This is not only clichéd, it can also look very stiff and awkward. As a simple variation, get people in the group to stand side-on to you and then turn their heads to face the camera. This is a more relaxed pose and will instantly give the image a more natural appearance. Also, try arranging people in different locations, such as in the bottom image on the facing page.

Another option for a group composition is to organize the subjects in different positions: standing, sitting, kneeling and even lying down. (If you plan this beforehand you can save time when it comes to shooting.) Props are also a good way of adding interest – give people something to hold or arrange them around nearby objects. Group shots need not be either staid nor conventional; the more inventive you are, the more the subjects will enjoy the experience and respond well.

Don't forget

Always take several group shots since there will invariably be someone blinking or looking the wrong way.

Capturing Activities

Although portrait shots of adults and children are great for framing and putting on the wall, more interesting images can be captured of people when they are involved in some form of activity. This could be something physical, such as playing sport, or something more contemplative, such as reading. Whatever the activity, this type of shot has the benefit that the subject is not usually posing and so it provides a more natural result than a formally posed image.

The first thing to do when capturing an activity shot is to select the activity and the appropriate surroundings. (In some cases it may just be a question of seeing a suitable shot, such as your child reading a book, and taking it immediately.) If possible, try and capture activities in their natural environment as this gives a general context to the activity.

Beware

When capturing activities make sure you have the correct camera settings already applied. This will save you from having to fiddle around with the camera when you could be capturing shots.

An important element of activity shots is the use of a zoom lens. This is because you should be a reasonable distance away from your subject so that you do not crowd them (as with the images on

> You should be a reasonable distance away from your subject so that you do not crowd them

the facing page). If possible, the subject should be unaware that you are there. To try and achieve this, find a suitable shooting position and stay there for a period of time so that you are not so noticeable to your subject.

When it comes to capturing a particular activity the camera settings will depend on the type of shot you are taking. For someone reading a book you may want to use a wide aperture (low f-number) to try and blur the background so that they stand out more. For a sporting activity, you may want to use a fast shutter speed to try and freeze the action. However, with any type of activity shot that involves movement there may be a bit of trial and error involved. But if you work out beforehand what you are trying to achieve you will be better placed to capture the image when the moment arrives.

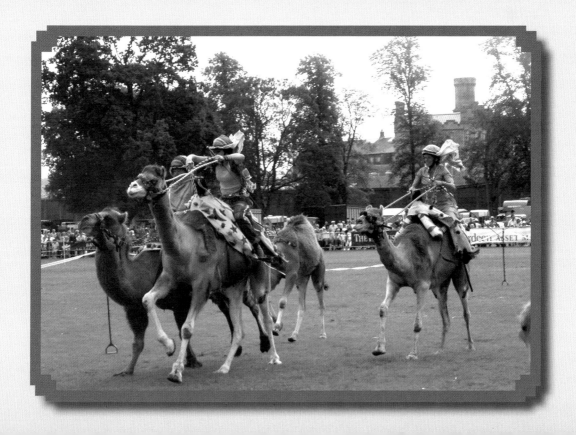

Candid Shots

A good portrait may adorn your wall or mantelpiece for many years and it is one of the most common ways to capture images of people. But unposed, or candid, shots can be just as appealing and they offer a different type of insight into the character of the subject.

The best way to capture candid shots is to ensure that the subject is unaware of your presence with a camera. If there are other people around you can try blending in with them, or place yourself behind an object such as a car or a pillar (but make sure it does not look as though you are spying on the subject). Another, perhaps better, option is to use a camera with a powerful zoom lens. This will enable you to stand far enough away from the subject so that they do not think you are trying to photograph them.

> The best way to capture candid shots is to ensure that the subject is unaware of your presence

Patience is the key when capturing candid shots; sometimes you will have to wait several minutes until you get the right image (since you cannot tell the subject what you want them to do). In some ways it is similar to capturing images of wildlife, in that you have to make yourself inconspicuous and then be prepared to wait.

The images on the facing page were taken with a zoom lens of 210mm. This allowed for enough space between the subjects and the photographer so that the subjects were concentrating on their activity rather than the photographer.

These shots benefit from not being static and they both convey a sense of action and also a certain trepidation. The reaction of the children is what makes the images interesting and conveys the emotion of the moment. The motion also ensures that their attention is completely diverted from the camera, thereby creating the unguarded pose.

Posed Options

One option for people shots is when individuals are deliberately posing for you, preferably with an interesting costume or act. In many tourist centers around the world, or at festivals, there are street performers who make excellent subjects for photographers. They are usually flamboyant characters with colorful costumes and props, so there is a lot of scope for experimentation. As with all people shots, take your time to get the best vantage point (this may involve waiting until the initial crowds have subsided) and try to get the subject in as interesting a pose as possible. Also, make sure you put some money in their hat or collecting bucket, if there is one, as then they may be more likely to create a specific pose for you.

Filling the Frame

An effective technique for capturing portraits is to fill the frame with as much of the subject's face as possible. This can create a very powerful effect since every feature of the face is detailed in the image. This type of image is frequently used for politicians and business people as it conveys a sense of control and it can also look slightly intimidating. Look at some newspapers and magazines to see how these types of images are used to illustrate certain types of story.

When capturing this type of shot it is vital to use a zoom lens and the bigger the better. To create the same effect without a zoom would result in you being only inches away from the subject's face, which is unlikely to result in a natural-looking image.

Initially, try zooming in so that there is still a slight border around the subject's face. Then, take another shot where their whole face fills the viewfinder or the LCD panel. Finally, try and take a shot so that only their main features are visible. Compare the three shots to see the different visual effects that they create.

> Take another shot where their whole face fills the viewfinder or the LCD panel

If you want to add extra emphasis to this type of shot this can be achieved by capturing the subject from below their eye line. If you shoot up towards someone and fill the frame, the resultant image will look as if they are towering over you, with all of their features clearly depicted.

Another option for this type of image is to convert it to black and white once it has been captured. The top image on the facing page conveys the sense of detail and expression in the features, while the bottom image has an extra dimension in black and white.

Black and White

Images can be converted to black and white in image editing software by removing the color from an image. Some cameras can also capture black and white images.

Children

There are probably more digital images captured of children than any other subject. Digital cameras are ideal for this purpose as you can take an almost limitless number of pictures and children can then immediately look at them to see the results. Children who grow up with digital cameras expect to be able to see the pictures on the camera's LCD panel and if they are ever faced with a film camera they may be perplexed because they cannot see the images.

One of the main problems when capturing images of children is that they tend to perform a passable impression of perpetual motion. They are rarely still for very long so it can be a challenge to try and capture effective images of them. Frequently when capturing images of children, you will take what you think is a perfect shot but they will have moved or blinked

Children tend to perform a passable impression of perpetual motion

just at the moment when the actual shot was taken. One way to try and overcome this is to use the continuous shooting mode whereby several shots can be taken consecutively. This means you will get a lot of similar shots and hopefully one of them will be effective as a portrait of the subject.

Portraits of children are familiar photographic subjects and there is absolutely nothing wrong with a standard, face-on portrait. However, in addition to this, try to capture portraits that offer something slightly different – put the children in an unusual or picturesque location or include additional elements in the image such as flowers or family pets. In the top image on the facing page the composition of the child and the rope ladder gives the portrait a different perspective and a more relaxed aspect.

Capturing images of children involved in an activity is an excellent option too. This is because their attention is diverted and there is also the activity itself to help make the image more interesting. In the bottom image on the facing page the activity of playing the violin gives a natural looking image as the child is concentrating rather than looking directly at the camera.

Hot tip

Let children practice with digital cameras as this helps them learn about photography and it also makes them more comfortable around cameras when it comes to capturing images of them.

Relaxed Portraits

When capturing portraits of either adults or children the biggest problem is the obvious presence of the camera, particularly if it is a posed, formal portrait. One partial solution is to use a zoom lens so that you are further away from the subject and they do not feel too pressurized by the camera. Also, try putting the camera on a tripod and use a remote control (if you have one) to activate the shutter release. This means that you can detach yourself from the camera and talk to the subject in a relaxed fashion. Be aware of your surroundings too and try and make them as inviting as possible: make sure the room is uncluttered and that the subject is comfortable.

One way to increase your chances of taking a poor portrait is to ask your subject to stand facing you directly. This is a pose that can make people feel awkward, as if they are almost standing to attention. Instead, ask the subject to sit in a relaxed way on a chair or ask them to stand side-on to you and then turn their head towards the camera. This is a more relaxed pose and should result in a more effective portrait.

Ask the subject to sit in a relaxed way on a chair or ask them to stand side-on to you and then turn their head towards the camera

Another factor when capturing portraits is to make the subject as relaxed as possible. Talk to them before you start taking pictures and tell them what you want to do. In some cases it will be beneficial to give the subject some type of prop (especially if children are involved). To try and capture the best facial expression, ask the subject to look down and close their eyes. Then, on the count of three, ask them to open their eyes and look up. If you capture the image at this point it should create a more natural expression as the subject will be less self-conscious.

8 Artistic Architecture

This chapter shows how to get the most out of photographing buildings. It looks at positioning, using the light and concentrating on certain elements of a building.

Finding the Right Spot

When capturing images of buildings and architecture there are a number of "standard" views. For instance, a straight-on shot of the Eiffel Tower or the Taj Mahal. These are instantly recognizable iconic images and it is always worth capturing a few of these if you are in this type of location. However, what you will end up with is essentially a picture postcard image. This is useful and effective for some purposes such as showing friends and relations but it is also advisable to try and capture some more creative shots to show a more individual side of a building.

When you are faced with a shot of a building or architecture the first thing to do is to take some of the conventional shots, just to make sure that you have got these taken care of. Even when you do this, try and avoid the crowds by capturing your images either early in the morning or later in the afternoon or evening.

Once you have captured the traditional shots you can then concentrate on finding a location from where you can capture more individual and artistic shots. The first thing to do is to walk around the building and look at it from every angle (depending on the building this may take some time but it is worth persevering with). Then you will be able to assess potential shots that show the building in a different context from the standard view. Look for close-ups to show the building's character, use the building's angles to show symmetry and patterns and change your own angle to alter the perspective (try getting above the building and also lying down and shooting from directly below part of the building).

The top image on the facing page is a "standard" one of the La Pedrera building in Barcelona, as it appears on many postcards. The bottom image is the same building but shot from much closer and directly from the pavement below, thereby highlighting the character of the building more.

Beware

Never put yourself in physical danger when trying to find the right spot for capturing images. Sometimes it is better to ignore a shot than to risk injury.

Concentrate on finding a location from where you can capture more individual and artistic shots

Capturing the Best Light

The Golden Hour is the time just after sunrise and just before sunset when the light has a rich, golden color which is perfect for photography (presuming the sun is out and there is not heavy cloud cover). Sometimes as a photographer you stumble across this type of light, but more often than not you have to make the effort to be in the right place at the right time to capture images with this type of light.

The first thing to do when trying to capture the best light is to check the times of sunrise and sunset. You can then decide on the location from where you want to capture images and work out when you need to be there in relation to the sunrise and sunset times. Make sure you are at your location at least half an hour (preferably one hour) before the ideal time you have calculated for photography. This is to allow yourself time to get set up and select potential shots and also to take some shots in the current lighting conditions so that you can compare these to the Golden Hour ones.

Make sure you are at your location at least half an hour before the ideal time you have calculated for photography

After checking the sunrise and sunset times you should then check the overall weather forecast; there may be little point in trying to capture the early morning or evening sun if it is going to be heavily overcast. The best sort of conditions are generally clear skies with some broken cloud. This should still allow the Golden Hour sun to illuminate your subjects and the cloud will provide additional color for sunsets and silhouettes.

Sometimes, even with diligent planning, you will come across the best light quite by chance. Both of the images on the facing page were captured about 20 minutes after it seemed the sun had gone down and disappeared. However, I waited another half an hour and the sun reappeared, allowing for these images with the rich, golden light.

Hot tip

Even if you think you have missed the best light it can still pay dividends to wait a few minutes to make sure that the sun is not going to reappear or there are not some other shots that can be captured.

126

Using the Angles

Many shots of buildings are taken as straight-on, two-dimensional images. While this can create highly effective photographs, it would be wrong to concentrate on this type of image exclusively. Buildings are frequently a fascinating combination of curves and angles that can create a much broader context for them.

All buildings have angles and these are a rich source of photographic opportunities. Angles can be used to emphasize the size of a building. The image on the facing page is an example of this. The size of the monument is emphasized by the angles of the structure and this gives it a completely different character from that seen in a straight-on shot from further away. For this it is essential to find the right spot from which to capture the angles of the building or structure.

The image on this page was created using the angles of the building by capturing it at 45 degrees from the corner. This gives a sense of perspective and the patterned effect that is achieved creates a more interesting image than a standard straight-on one.

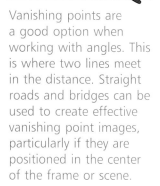

Hot tip

Vanishing points are a good option when working with angles. This is where two lines meet in the distance. Straight roads and bridges can be used to create effective vanishing point images, particularly if they are positioned in the center of the frame or scene.

Emphasizing Size

Using the size of a building or piece of architecture is an excellent way to display its context. Different techniques can be used to show the imposing nature of a building, or represent it as a small part of its surrounding area. Either way, it is a useful option for revealing some of the character of a building.

As shown on the previous page the size of a building can be emphasized by capturing an image from directly below it. This creates a sense of perspective and can be used to exaggerate the size of a structure.

Another option for emphasizing the size of an object is to capture it against a plain background, so that it stands out against its surroundings. If there are other objects in the picture that can be used to contrast with the size of the building then so much the better. In the image below the stature of the cranes serves to show the comparatively diminutive size of the structure below, while they create an eye-catching composition in their own right. In the image on the facing page the plain background serves to emphasize the imposing nature of the structure, as does the inclusion of a lot of smaller buildings in the background.

Concentrating on Details

By their very nature most buildings are made out of numerous small elements that are combined to create the whole structure. However, frequently when we capture images we concentrate on the overall building rather than its constituent parts. This can be a great oversight as there is a wealth of photographic material in the detail of buildings.

Details help to convey the character of buildings, rather than their overall appearance. This can cover a multitude of elements: windows, door handles, artwork, tiles and stone structures. In fact, almost anything that is part of a building.

A useful way to capture detail in a building is to start from a distance from where you can capture the whole building and then work your way closer and closer to capture the details. This can be used as a series of images to show different aspects of the same structure, and each of the images should be able to stand up in its own right as well.

The image below is a long-distance shot of a building with a number of modern design features. The top image on the facing page shows the details of one particular side of the building. The bottom image on the facing page is a close-up of a single window within the wall above. This reveals some of the design features of the building and provides an interesting contrast to the long-distance image.

Don't forget

Building details are excellent for conveying textures and design features.

Using Patterns

Patterns are all around us: natural patterns, artificial patterns, symmetrical patterns and asymmetrical patterns. Whenever you have a camera with you it is always a good habit to look for images that contain patterns.

When capturing patterns it is usually best to use a zoom lens so that the pattern can fill as much of the frame as possible. This gives the pattern added impact as there are no other elements in the image to detract from it.

Patterns can be used to highlight a certain feature or characteristic of a subject or they can be used in their own right just as an artistic image. The image below displays an irregular pattern of scaffolding that conveys the industrial nature of the structure. By using a zoom lens the complexity of the structure is displayed, showing the way in which the elements in the pattern interact.

The top image on the facing page is a pattern that stands on its own and it is given an extra dimension through the use of color in the window boxes. The bottom image on the facing page is a symmetrical pattern that serves to convey the ornate character of the building. By concentrating on this type of pattern the image helps to demonstrate the ordered and artistic nature of the structure. Sometimes, close-up patterns can reveal more about a building than a wide-angle shot.

Foreground Elements

Architecture shots can be both dramatic and artistic. Sometimes an image of a building itself is enough to create a compelling photograph. The size and character of a building can frequently be captured in an image without any additional elements and this is always a good option for buildings.

Even though images of buildings on their own can be effective there are times when it is a good idea to include other objects in the foreground of the image. This can serve to give context to the image (for instance, a national flag in an image can create a geographical context) or just to brighten up what would be a good, but not stunning, image.

Foreground objects do not have to dominate the image and sometimes "less is more" is a good maxim for this type of shot.

Sometimes "less is more" is a good maxim for this type of shot

In the top image on the facing page the flowers in the foreground only take up a small proportion of the picture but the eye is immediately drawn to them because of the vibrant colors. This leads you into the image and after the foreground object has been noticed the eye is then drawn to the main subject. Without the flowers, the image would have been a fairly unexceptional one.

The bottom image on the facing page has a greater emphasis on the foreground objects, in this case the trees. This shot was taken as one of a series of images, some of which included foreground objects and some which did not. The inclusion of the foreground trees gives a better sense of the building's location and provides a contrast to the modern architecture.

Options

Some of the types of objects that can be included in the foreground of an architecture shot include trees, plants, statues, street lamps, vehicles and even people. Take time to compose the objects in relation to the building.

Dealing with Distortion

One problem with lenses in digital cameras is that the glass is slightly curved. In certain conditions this can result in elements within an image looking distorted. This tends to be particularly obvious in images of buildings. The problems can also be made worse if a zoom lens is used. In the image below the church spire appears at an angle, although this is an optical effect caused by the camera lens. Since the spire is at the side of the image (where the lens is most curved) the distortion has been made worse. Always check images of buildings to see if they look distorted or at an angle. If this is the case then there are some steps that can be taken to try and reduce the distortion.

If your images of buildings suffer from distortion there are a few options for trying to rectify this. One is to position the main subject in the center of the frame rather than at one of the sides. Another step is to move further away from the subject – the closer you are, the more pronounced the distortion. If you are further away from the subject then the curve of the lens will be more forgiving. Similarly, if there is already distortion in an image, the use of zoom will exaggerate this even further.

Another option for removing distortion is to use a dedicated architecture lens. This is a specialist lens that is designed to eliminate the curvature of the lens. However, these types of lenses tend to be expensive but if you are taking a lot of architecture photography these types of lenses may be worth looking at.

9 Capturing Landscapes

This chapter looks at landscapes and details ways in which you can bring them to life with different techniques and approaches.

Creating Your Scene

In some cases, stunning landscape images will come to you: a beautiful sunrise or sunset, or a desert landscape highlighted by a single, lone tree. However, on other occasions you will have to put a bit more effort into your shots and actively go out and create a scene with the elements at your disposal.

One way to create effective scenes is to combine existing elements, such as natural landscapes and constructed objects. If you are doing this, try and locate the constructed element first and then work this into the composition. The image below was created in this way. The line of benches had to be captured at a specific angle to ensure that they formed a line to draw the viewer's eye through the image. Without the benches the image would have been unremarkable. With the images on the facing pages the natural elements in the scene (i.e. the trees) have helped to create the final composition of the images.

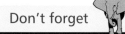

Don't forget

It may be permissible to move objects within a scene, or add them to a scene if necessary. However, make sure you are not interfering with anything else and always replace any objects that you use in your scene.

140

Creating Moods

It is not essential to use the Golden Hour to capture images in good photographic lighting conditions. All types of lighting can be used to capture images and the only constraint is your own imagination. When different lighting conditions are available they can be used to create different types of mood within an image.

Low-level or dull lighting is often thought of as being non-conducive to good photographs. However, this can be an excellent opportunity to capture atmospheric images. This type of light usually has an even quality, so different exposure levels throughout the image become less of an issue. Frequently on cloudy days an hour or so before sunset this type of light can be used to produce very natural-looking images. The top image on the facing page was captured in the late evening on a cloudy day and it helps to

Low-level lighting can be an excellent opportunity to capture atmospheric images

create a mood of tranquility and serenity. Due to the lighting levels a tripod was used to keep the camera steady, since a shutter speed of 1/15th second was needed to maintain a narrow aperture for a large depth of field – to keep as much of the image in focus as possible.

A change in the weather is another opportunity for creating mood images. For instance, the dark clouds of an incoming storm make a dramatic backdrop to landscape images and can be used to emphasize the power of nature in an image. An approaching rain storm is ideal for conveying the mood of changing weather.

Snow scenes also offer valuable opportunities for conveying a sense of mood. In the bottom image on the facing page the snow has helped to produce an atmospheric scene, that is enhanced by the lack of people. Again this image was captured with a wide aperture and a slow shutter speed, in order to capture as much detail as possible and achieve the desired lighting conditions.

Beware

If you are capturing images of storms this can be most effective just before the storm breaks. Try and get indoors before the storm itself arrives.

Including Objects of Interest

The human eye is naturally drawn to objects or items that stand out in an image. For instance, a contrasting color or an unusual object will catch the eye, especially within landscape scenes. When dealing with landscapes it is always a good idea to try and look for objects of interest and include them in the scene in some way.

Objects of interest can include almost anything depending on the scene. For instance, a red flower in a field of white ones will catch the attention, as will an incongruous object in a landscape scene, such as a lone house amongst a range of hills.

Aim to try and create a "road map" that can guide the viewer through the image

When using objects of interest within a scene the aim is to try and create a "road map" that can guide the viewer through the image. Ideally, they should notice the object of interest first and then be able to follow their way through the rest of the image from there.

In the top image on the facing page, the bridge structure acts as the initial object of interest. The eye is then drawn to the landscape behind the bridge and this creates an image that would have been fairly standard without the bridge in it. This type of image can frequently be captured in the country and so it is always good to get into the habit of searching for buildings or structures when you are in this type of location.

The bottom image on the facing page contains a smaller object of interest, the flowerbed in front of the monument. Although this is a small part of the image it is enhanced by the color and the prominence in the foreground and creates an interesting road map. The eye is initially drawn to the front of the image to the flowers. It then travels up to the main element of the image, the monument. Even though the object of interest is relatively small in this scene it still catches the attention because of the color contrast with the background and the rest of the image.

Story Telling

Some photographic locations offer the chance for one single, stunning image. However, in most cases, there are numerous opportunities for capturing a variety of images. Even if you cannot immediately see the chance for different images it is always worthwhile looking around a location to see if you can capture a range of shots. Once you have perfected this you should be able to create a photo essay in almost any situation. This is a collection of images that together give a sense of the character of a location.

Wherever you are with your camera try and think of the different types of shots that are available. For instance, if you are on holiday on the beach you may take some family shots of people playing in the sand. But then have a look at the sea and the waves and try to capture some artistic shots by stopping the water or giving it the appearance of motion. Then take a walk along the beach and look in rock pools for any signs of life. Also, take some texture shots of the rocks and plants themselves. Finally, at the end of the day capture some social shots of people leaving the beach, to contrast with the action and enjoyment of earlier in the day. Look at the obvious and then try and enhance this with as many different types of shots as possible. The end result will create a much more interesting collection.

The collection of images on the following pages was captured at Barcelona Harbour, to try and show all of the different characteristics of this area.

Don't forget

Look at all of the elements in a scene to see how each one can be best used to improve the overall composition of the image.

Hot tip

Generally, for story-telling images, set the camera to aperture priority mode and select an aperture of f16 or f22 to ensure that as much of the image as possible is in focus.

Bands of Color

Color is all around us and the human eye can differentiate millions of different colors and shades. In photographic terms, color is an essential ingredient, but it is not always necessary to include as many colors as possible for effective images. It is always good practice to think about color in images and the best way in which it can be used.

One way to use color in images is to show an extravagant or vibrant event such as a festival or a carnival. Colorful costumes and designs can then be used to capture a flavor of the event and it is an excellent way to get some very striking images.

Another, perhaps more understated, way of using color is to look for large blocks of color in a scene and see if they can be incorporated into a meaningful image. Bands of color can be used either horizontally or vertically: three good options are the sky, the sea and grassed areas such as fields and parks.

The use of bands of color can be made to highlight other items in the image by creating a "sandwich" effect. This is where the bands of color are above and below the main subject. This displays the center area as the filling in the sandwich, while the colored areas are still noteworthy in their own right. This is the case in the top image on the facing page, where the blue sky and green park act as the two areas of color that are highlighting the band in the center of the image.

> **Bands of color can be made to highlight other items in the image by creating a "sandwich" effect**

Bands of color are just as effective if they are used vertically, as in the bottom image on the facing page, where the green of one side of the field contrasts with the yellow–golden appearance of the other half. With this type of scene it is important to locate yourself in the right position, so that the line between the two bands of color is in the middle. This will split the colored bands and also draw the viewer's eye through the middle of the image to the back.

Panoramas

Digital cameras have proved to be very successful and popular at creating panoramas. These are two or more images of a scene that is too large to be captured in a single shot. The successive images are stitched together to give one panoramic image. Panoramas can be created in image editing software programs and a lot of digital cameras also have a facility for creating them within the camera.

When capturing images for a stitched panoramic scene make sure that you capture the different images from the same location and at the same exposure settings. If possible, use a tripod to ensure the same point of shooting and overlap each image by approximately 20% so that the stitching appears seamless.

Another way to create panoramas is to capture an image and then crop it so that it appears in a panoramic format. In order to do this, capture the image at the camera's highest possible resolution. This will enable you to crop the image and still print it out at a large size. The panorama across these two pages was created in this way, with the source image being the top one on the facing page. This serves to isolate one part of the image and create a panoramic effect because of its dimensions.

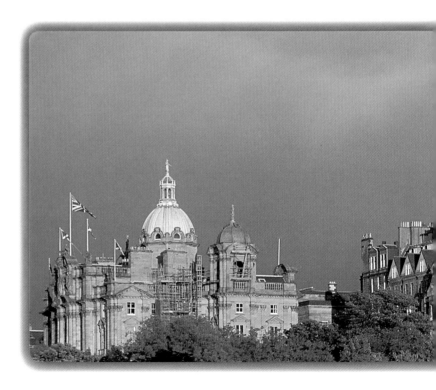

Reflections

One of the great qualities of water is that it creates reflections and these can be incorporated into photographs in a variety of ways. The most obvious way is in the reflection of landscapes or objects such as buildings or bridges that are located near water.

The classic reflection shot is one where the water is very still so that the object and its reflection look as similar as possible, as in the image below. Lakes are the best for this type of shot. Ideally, try visiting them on a day when there is very little wind. With faster-moving water, such as streams and rivers, it is still perfectly possible to get good reflection shots. This creates a rippled effect in the reflection and, as long as it is not too extreme, this can result in a very pleasing image.

Another option for reflection shots is to take a more proactive role and deliberately create artistic effects. One way to do this is to throw a stone into a pool or lake and then capture the shot including the resulting ripples.

10 Using Motion Creatively

Movement can be hazardous to photography but this chapter shows how to harness speed in different ways.

Stopping Water

Water is one of the great substances for photography. It can take on different forms such as snow and ice; it can be static or moving; it can be used for reflections; it can take on different colors and textures (ripples); and it can be rendered in different ways using various photographic techniques. Overall it can be one of the most satisfying photographic subjects.

One photographic technique for water is showing how to freeze its motion. Not in the form of ice but rather a photographic freezing to create the appearance of the water having almost stopped in mid air. This can be done with any type of moving water, such as a stream, a waterfall, a hose or even a water slide.

The trick to making water freeze in an image is to use a fast shutter speed. To do this you will have to set your camera to shutter speed priority. This means that you can set the shutter speed and the camera will select an appropriate aperture. Select a shutter speed of at least 1/500th second, which should be fast enough to capture the water as it is falling but before it has moved too far. If there is enough light, and if your camera will allow it, you can use shutter speeds in the range of 1/2000th second. The image below was taken with a shutter speed of 1/1000th second, which resulted in a relatively wide aperture of f5.6. Due to the fast shutter speed the water is captured very quickly so that the individual drops are visible.

Beware

Always keep your camera far away from water. If it gets wet it will almost certainly stop working. If this happens, dry it out completely before you try and use it again as this will increase the chances of it recovering fully.

Blurring Water

The opposite photographic technique to stopping water is making it blurred to convey a sense of motion. This can produce soft, almost cloud-like images that are very soothing and comforting. The best options for this are large waves, waterfalls and fast-moving streams or rivers.

When capturing images of blurred water you should use a tripod so that you can use shutter speeds that are slow enough to create the blurred effect. Start by setting the camera to shutter speed priority and use an initial shutter speed of 1/30th second to see the result. Then take the shot again several times, each time making the shutter speed one stop slower (the image below was taken with a shutter speed of 1/6th second). One drawback with this is that as the shutter speed gets slower, so more light enters the camera, even with the aperture at its narrowest setting. Depending on the amount of available light, there will probably come a point when the shutter speed is too slow, resulting in the image being over-exposed, i.e. too much light entering the camera. Because of this, the best time to capture blurred water images is on an overcast day when the natural light is not too bright.

Once you have mastered capturing images of blurred water you may want to start actively searching out water scenes so that you can experiment further with this technique.

Capturing Speed

Showing the impression of speed in a still image is obviously something of a challenge. By its very nature, digital photography is a static medium, but this is not to say that it is impossible to convey the idea of speed. This can be done for any fast moving object: vehicles, animals and people.

One way that the impression of speed is depicted in photography is to show the moving object against a blurred background. This serves to create the idea of speed by showing that the object is moving so quickly that the background cannot be caught in focus. The trick here is to ensure that the moving object is in sharper focus than the background and this is done by using a technique called panning.

Panning works by following a moving object in the viewfinder of the camera and then capturing the image while the moving camera is still following the object. For instance, if a vehicle is moving from point A to point C, via point B, this can be used for the panning technique. Start following the vehicle at point A and capture the image at point B, but make sure the camera moves with the vehicle the whole way.

Panning can be used on any moving object, such as vehicles and people.

Hot tip

A similar effect to panning is known as tilting. This is when the camera follows a vertically moving object (such as a rocket) rather than a horizontal one.

158

Hot tip

Use AI Servo focus when capturing moving objects. This will track the object as it is moving to ensure it is in focus.

Blurring Speeding Objects

Creating a blurred effect for speeding objects is similar to capturing blurred images of water: a slow shutter speed is required to enable the speeding object to become blurred. However, since objects such as vehicles, and people, are usually faster than water the technique is slightly different.

When creating blurred effects for vehicles, animals or people there are two options. The first is to create an image that is universally blurred; the second is to have a blurred object over a sharp background. This is created by panning the camera on the speeding object, but not focusing. This results in the whole image being blurred, which can create a slightly surreal impression of speed, depending on the object in the image.

The other way to capture blurred speeding objects is to use a slow shutter speed and, holding the camera still, let them move past the camera. The shutter speed should not be too slow, otherwise they would move through the frame before the shot was completed. The image below was captured at a shutter speed of 1/60th second which was just fast enough so that the camera could be hand-held without the need for a tripod.

Don't forget

To blur images of vehicles, a faster shutter speed can usually be used than for blurring images of people, since vehicles will probably be moving faster.

Continuous Shooting

When dealing with shots involving motion it is not uncommon to wish that you could take several shots in a row, to capture the action at split-second intervals. With digital SLRs this can be achieved by using the Continuous Shooting mode. This is usually accessed from the Drive menu, where the options include Single, Continuous and Self-Timer.

Continuous shooting is measured in frames per second, i.e. the number of shots the camera can take in this mode in one second. The lowest level will be about 3 frames per second, going up to approximately 8 frames per second depending on the type of digital SLR. To capture continuous shots you have to select this option either from a button on the camera body or from the camera's internal menu system. Once this has been done you use the Continuous Shooting mode in the same way as taking a single shot: half-depress the shutter release button to focus the image and then fully depress it to capture the shot. In Continuous mode the camera will keep capturing images until you take your finger off the shutter release button.

In continuous mode the camera will keep capturing images until you take your finger off the shutter release button

Don't forget

Different focus settings can be applied when using Continuous Shooting. For instance, if you are photographing moving objects the AI Servo autofocus setting can be used. This will focus on the moving object for each consecutive shot.

Continuous shooting can be used in any photographic situation but it is most effective in shots involving action such as sports shots. Sometimes the action is too fast to guarantee capturing a perfect image in a single shot and with continuous shooting your chances of getting the shot you want increase significantly. It is also good for producing a series of action images, as with the series of photographs on the facing page.

Continuous shooting can also be a good option for capturing portraits, particularly of children, who tend to move more during the photographic process. If you use continuous shooting then there is more chance of capturing an acceptable image even if the child is blinking, talking or moving.

Creating Ghostly Shadows

Trick photography has been around for as long as cameras themselves. With the advent of digital cameras and image editing software this has been taken to a level where we can no longer be sure that a digital image is a genuine, unadulterated original or not. But within digital SLRs it is still possible to create original images with a trick element, without the need to resort to software wizardry. One of these tricks is the creation of ghostly shadows in an image.

To create effective shadows of people in an image you will need a tripod and a dark night. Set up the tripod near an area where there are a reasonable number of people. Try and ensure that the overall composition of the image is good too so that you do not have to rely solely on the people in the image. Then, set the camera to shutter speed priority mode and set the shutter speed to a minimum of 10 seconds (the longer the exposure time, the more shadows you will achieve). Once you have activated the shutter release button the people who pass the camera will be captured as shadowy outlines, as in the image below. Try and ensure that there are some people who are standing still, too, to give more solid-looking images. This technique can also be used for two people: get one to stand still and the other to move through the image to play the part of the ghost.

Don't forget

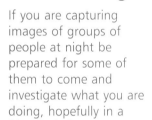

If you are capturing images of groups of people at night be prepared for some of them to come and investigate what you are doing, hopefully in a friendly fashion.

11 Effective Composition

This chapter concentrates on how to compose a scene using different photographic techniques.

Rule of Thirds

An image can be improved by having the main subject away from the center of the image. This can give it a more natural appearance and make it look less posed. However, it is not just a case of positioning the subject anywhere out of the center of the image, which could result in an unbalanced picture. Instead imagine your image as a grid of 3 x 3 squares and position your subject at the intersection point of any of the grid lines or in one of the subsequent sectors (see below). This should provide you with an eye-catching and balanced composition.

This is known as the "rule of thirds" and it can be applied to give an image a completely different perspective. Always keep this in mind when you are capturing images and experiment with the subject in different areas of the rule of thirds grid. In the three images on the facing page the composition of the pictures has been altered considerably by moving the main subject to different points in the rule of thirds grid.

Don't forget

Sometimes the best shot is to have the main subject in the center of the frame, so always consider this as an option too.

Moving the Horizon

A similar technique to the rule of thirds is that of moving the horizon. This is simply a case of repositioning the camera so that the horizon appears at different places in each shot. If you do this then you can have three shots with the horizon at the top, middle and bottom of the image. This can be achieved by moving the camera very slightly up or down between shots. Only a small adjustment is required to create dramatically different scenes from shot to shot.

Moving the horizon can be applied to landscape shots, but also those with other objects, such as buildings. It is always worth trying to move the horizon, even if you end up using a standard shot with the horizon in the middle of the shot.

The image below has placed the main subject in the top third of the image. This gives greater prominence to the foreground. The image on the facing page has the main subject in the bottom third of the image. This gives it a more expansive appearance because of the increased amount of sky. Both of these shots were captured from the same point and create different viewpoints by altering the position of the horizon.

Framing a Scene

The first thing that many of us do with a pleasing photographic image is to put it in a frame to show it at its best. This is a normal reaction but it is also possible to use elements in scenes to act as frames within the image itself. This serves to emphasize part of an image and provides an extra artistic element to the picture.

When looking for items to use as frames within images the list is extensive: doorways, arches, branches, bridges, holes and pillars are just a few. The trick is to position yourself so that the frame is in the correct position and not obscuring a significant part of the image itself. The frame object should also be thought of as an important part of the image. It can be placed around the very border of the image or it can be a central part of the image in its own right. In the image below the window opening acts as a frame for the background but it is still an important element of the image. In the top image on the facing page the statue acts as a frame for the lamp behind it, but at this distance the statue is still the main object. In the bottom image on the facing page, a close-up of the statue serves to better frame the lamp and the depth of field highlights the distance between the two objects.

Still Life

Still life images are perhaps more commonly associated with paintings but it is a subject that should not be overlooked for photographic images. In simple terms, a still life is an image of a collection of inanimate objects. These can be arranged in an artistic or a humorous way and the end result is frequently in the eye of the beholder.

Creating still life images can be an art in itself and it is sometimes easier to find still life scenes that other people have created and then use these in your images. Good areas to look at are businesses that are trying to attract people into their premises, as this is often done with eye-catching still life designs. Shops, restaurants, cafés and pubs often have still life displays near their doorways; it is usually better to look around areas with smaller, more specialized outlets rather than large malls or shopping centers. The image on the facing page was captured outside a café in France. The combination of fruit, lighting and background creates an evocative scene that captures the essence of the establishment.

If you want to create your own still life images you will first have to create the still life itself. This may depend on your artistic ability but try and follow a few general rules. Base your still life scenes on single themes, such as food, art, sport or technology. This is not to say that you cannot have unconnected objects for emphasis but try and choose the majority of the items from the same general group. Then arrange the items so that they can all be viewed (or at least parts of them can). Keep smaller objects more towards the front and larger ones at the back and try to aim for an even composition, i.e. one in which nothing looks out of place. The element on which the still life is placed is also important: there is little point having a well-crafted still life that is on an incongruously shabby table. Treat every element in the still life as a crucial one.

The final thing to think about before you photograph the still life is the lighting. You may need to add extra lighting to illuminate different parts of the scene. If possible, make it portable so that you can position it as required in natural lighting.

Hot tip

Still life images can be captured in a wider context in addition to the objects themselves. For instance, a still life within a shop window shows that it is serving a specific purpose, i.e. trying to attract customers.

Subjects

Fruit, vegetables and flowers make excellent subjects for still life images and all three can be combined.

Waiting for the Right Shot

As with anything, luck plays its part in good photography. Sometimes a perfect image will just present itself in front of you. Unfortunately this is a rare event, but you can increase your chances of it happening by trying to be in the right place at the right time. Try planning the shot that you want to take and be in the correct position to take advantage of it when it comes along.

By definition, waiting for the right shot to come along can take time but it definitely pays to be patient and stay at a location for as long as you can. The image below is a good example of this. I was capturing images of car lights but decided to wait a bit longer, just in case something more interesting came along. After half an hour, a maintenance truck went past with several tail-lights on the back of its safety sign. The resultant image is slightly different from a standard tail-light one. This was a case of making my own luck through waiting long enough.

Don't forget

If you are waiting for a specific shot, do not give up just because you do not capture it first time. Go back at the next available opportunity and try again; some of the most satisfying images are those that require a bit of work.

12 Unusual Conditions

Different lighting or environmental conditions can be very rewarding for photographers. This chapter details a few of the options that are available for these types of shots.

Fireworks

The combination of color, patterns and movement is a captivating one in photographs and this is rarely better displayed than through fireworks. Fireworks displays are increasingly common, particularly on major holidays such as national holidays, Thanksgiving and New Year. For photography, organized displays are best as they usually go on for the longest time and have the best range of fireworks (and since you do not have to organize anything you can concentrate on capturing images rather than setting off pyrotechnics).

If you are going to be capturing fireworks images at an organized display, try and arrive early so that you can get to the best location. Since you will be shooting at night, you will need a tripod to keep the camera steady. Although you will be operating in low-level lighting, fireworks photography can include a variety of different shutter speeds.

At an organized display, try and arrive early so that you can get to the best location

Experiment with a fast shutter speed (approximately 1/60th or 1/125th second) to see if you can capture individual fireworks going off. The reason that a relatively fast speed can be used at night is that the fireworks themselves give off enough light for some interesting effects to be created.

Generally, slightly slower shutter speeds will create a more artistic effect and capture the sense of both color and motion. The images on the facing page were captured with a shutter speed of 1/4 second, which captures the fireworks as they explode and move through the sky.

Sparklers

Sparklers are another option for fireworks images as these tend to leave interesting trails of light.

Another way of capturing fireworks is to use a long exposure by setting the shutter speed to between five and ten seconds. This will enable you to capture several exploding fireworks in the same shot and it is very effective with a wide angle lens from a distance.

174

Car Tail Lights

Images of car tail-lights at night are a very satisfying exercise for night photography. The colored streaks that are created convey a sense of motion while producing images that have a surreal quality about them.

When trying to capture car tail-lights at night, select a location where you know there will be enough cars passing by. Depending on the time of year, you may be able to capture images during the rush hour, if the sun has gone down already. Make sure you are not physically on the road and use a tripod to keep the camera steady since you will be using a very slow shutter speed.

The trick with car tail-lights is to have a long enough exposure so that the vehicles have time to pass through the whole of the frame, causing the colored streaks to go into the distance. In the image below, the aperture was set to f16 to get as large a depth of field (as much of the image in focus) as possible. The shutter speed was set to 10 seconds so that the lights were caught throughout the image, but the moving vehicles were not visible as they were moving too quickly to be captured during this length of exposure. If cars are moving away from the camera the lights will be red and if they are moving towards the camera the lights will be white.

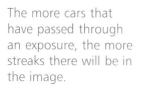

Don't forget

The more cars that have passed through an exposure, the more streaks there will be in the image.

Capturing Food

Food is another area that occupies a specialized niche in the professional market, but there is no reason why anyone with a digital camera cannot take impressive images of food and food-related items.

When dealing with food try to capture the essence of a particular type of food: the rich texture of chocolate by using a close-up shot, the freshness of an apple by cutting into it and showing the juice lying on the skin, or the size of a hot dog by photographing it length-on and at a low angle so that it fills the frame.

Try and create a sense of the dining experience rather than just the food on its own

It is also important to make an entire food scene as enticing as possible. If you are photographing a Thanksgiving Dinner for instance, include items such as the table setting, candles and flowers so that an overall ambience can be created. Try and create a sense of the dining experience rather than just the food on its own.

One valuable trick when capturing images of food is to do it when it is cold. This means that there will be no steam to cloud up the camera lens. Instead, try covering items with oil, or even wax, to give them that glistening appearance as if they are just out of the oven.

If you do capture food as it is being prepared, be careful not to get too close to saucepans and frying pans. This is because water or fat could splash onto the camera lens and spoil the shot, and potentially the camera too. Keep your distance and use a zoom lens to make the items look closer.

Spray it on

Fruit and vegetables can look a lot more enticing with water sprayed on them. This conveys a feeling of freshness, as if the produce has been picked in the early morning dew.

Water at Night

The photographic possibilities of water are increased once night falls and the opportunities for capturing images of water in the dark arise.

The crucial factor when capturing images of water at night is the use of a tripod. Due to the low levels of light, a shutter speed of several seconds will be required to allow enough light to enter the camera. If a tripod is not used the whole image will be blurred.

The use of a slow shutter speed has a significant impact on the appearance of the water in the final image. Since the water is still moving while the shutter is open this will create a blurred effect that takes on a soft, milky appearance. As long as there is some source of light this technique can create some stunningly atmospheric images. The image below was taken with an aperture of f8 and a shutter speed of 30 seconds. The scene was dimly lit by the moon, which provided enough light to give the moving water a bluish tinge. The images on the facing page were captured at f5.6 with a shutter speed of 10 seconds. This is because the lighting from the bridge provided more illumination so the shutter speed could be shorter than in the image below.

Hot tip

Experiment with longer and shorter shutter speeds to see the impact this has on both the lighting in a scene and the appearance of the water in it.

Illuminating Buildings

Shots of buildings during the day can be very satisfying and effective, but there is something about buildings at night that can give them a more glamorous and exciting appearance. In cities and towns around the world there are buildings that are illuminated at night and this presents them in an ideal condition for photography.

When capturing buildings at night, select ones that have some form of artificial lighting to illuminate them. This will give them the required lighting to make them stand out against their background. Another thing to remember with images of buildings at night is not to use the flash. This is because most flash units are not powerful enough to illuminate something as large as a building and they will only light up a small part of the foreground instead. (Flash can be used, but only if you are taking a close-up of one specific part of a building.)

Hot tip

Always bracket exposures when capturing night shots. This involves using exposure compensation either one or two stops above or below the exposure settings selected by the camera.

180

For images of buildings at night a tripod is essential. Because of the low levels of light, a slow shutter speed will be required so a tripod will be needed to keep the camera steady. As with any type of building image, try and capture the image from a spot where you can include the whole building and also foreground objects, if there are any. The top image on the facing page was captured with a shutter speed of two seconds in order to get enough light into the camera. Since the building was well illuminated, the shutter speed did not have to be any slower than this. The image is improved by the laser show that was taking place from the roof and it is always worth investigating if there are any buildings with light shows near where you are (a lot of major cities around the world have this type of event).

> A slow shutter speed will be required so a tripod will be needed to keep the camera steady

Details of buildings can also be captured at night. These are frequently illuminated by individual spotlights, as with the bottom image on the facing page. This image required a shutter speed of only one second since there was a reasonable amount of light from the spotlights, but at this length of exposure a tripod is still definitely needed.

Cityscapes at Night

When night falls this should not be the time to pack cameras away. In fact the opposite is true as this can be the time to capture stunning images. One popular option is cityscapes at night, when the buildings are illuminated and the street lights provide an additional source of light. If you are planning to do this, take some time out during the day to find potential locations and compositions as this will save you a lot of time and effort when it gets dark.

In the same way that the best light for daytime photography occurs an hour after sunrise and an hour before sunset, so the best time for night photography can be one hour after sunset. This produces a dusky light that still has some color in the sky from the reflected sun. This is known as an after-light and is frequently a dark purple in color, which can provide rich backdrops for cityscapes.

A group of buildings can convey the character of a city

One option when capturing cityscapes is to concentrate on a group of buildings. This can convey the character of a city and groups of skyscrapers are ideal for this, as in the top image on the facing page, which shows the Las Vegas depiction of New York skyscrapers. For this type of shot, use a wide-angle lens and a slow shutter speed. In this example, a shutter speed of 8 seconds was used, with the camera on a tripod.

Another option for cityscapes at night is to find a location that serves to capture its overall character, as shown in the bottom image on the facing page. To do this you may have to walk around a bit until you find the best location. Again, use a tripod and a slow shutter speed: the bottom image on the facing page was taken with a narrow aperture (f16) to create a large depth of field and a shutter speed of 15 seconds.

Be Careful

Take care when photographing cities at night and try not to look too conspicuous.

Snow Scenes

Initially it may seem that images of snow are simple to capture: you compose the scene and then snap away to create numerous winter scenes. This is true to a certain extent, but the problem is that, unless some corrective action is taken, the images will appear with gray snow, rather than the more traditional white. This is to do with how a digital camera measures light.

By default, internal light meters in digital cameras work by seeing everything as a "neutral gray". This means that they work out the correct light in a scene by calculating the amount of light reflected back to the camera as if all subjects were a neutral gray color. This is because neutral gray reflects approximately 18% of the light that hits it and this is the optimal level for measuring light in most photographic scenes. This is also known as 18% reflectance.

The problem with 18% reflectance and neutral gray is when it comes in contact with pure black or white. This is because they reflect either a lot less or a lot more light: black reflects approximately 9% of light and white reflects approximately 36% of light. What this means for capturing snow is that the camera will render it as 18% reflectance rather than 36%, which means the snow will appear as a neutral gray rather than white.

There are two options for capturing genuine white snow. One way is to take a normal metering reading and then use exposure compensation to add more light into the scene (one or two stops of exposure compensation is enough). Another option is to take a light meter reading from a non-white area of the scene. This will create a correct exposure and the scene can then be recomposed and captured. In the top image on the facing page the meter reading was taken from the blue sky just above the trees. This ensured that the exposure would be correct for the whole image once the scene was recomposed.

Once the metering for snow scenes has been mastered you can then concentrate on the composition. This can involve a scene of fresh snow, in which case it is always advisable to include at least one other object for interest. In some cases, as in the bottom image on the facing page, it sometimes pays to get out and about as the snow is falling as this can produce dramatic images. However, make sure you keep the camera dry.

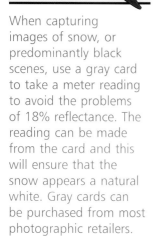

"Zoomed" Images

A lot of special photographic effects can be created through the use of image editing software. However, it is still possible for photographers to create some effects of their own while images are being captured. One of these is the effect of creating a "zoomed" image (see the example below).

In this context a zoomed image is one in which the zoom on the camera is moved as the shot is being captured. The easiest way to do this is with a digital SLR camera and a zoom lens of at least 18–70mm.

To create a zoomed image the camera has to be on a tripod, since a slow shutter speed will be used. Select an interesting subject and frame it in the middle of the viewfinder. Set the camera to shutter speed priority and select a shutter speed of at least 1/2 second. Focus the image and press the shutter release button. Simultaneously, zoom the lens from its longest focal length to its shortest (this is why a long shutter speed is required, to allow you enough time to zoom the lens). It will probably take a few attempts to get the timing right and you should try different shutter speeds to see how this affects the image. Also, try zooming from the shortest focal length to the longest to see the type of image that this produces.

Hot tip

Zoomed images can also be used for people, to create a sense of action and speed.

(13) Inspiring Techniques

Get started like a Pro!

Having a passion for photography is a good start to taking great photos. This chapter looks at some ways to fire this passion.

Think Like a Photographer

When you take photos with a digital SLR people will look at you and think that you are more serious about your photography than someone who takes snapshots. If you want to maintain this image, and take the best photos possible, then you should start thinking like a photographer. Some points to consider:

- Check out your locations. Sometimes as a photographer you stumble across the perfect location quite by accident. However, on most occasions it pays off to spend some time investigating locations to find out the best place from where to capture images and also the best time of day to do so in terms of light

- Use the best light. Although it is not always convenient, the best light for taking photos is first thing in the morning and just before dusk. Therefore you may have to make more of an effort to ensure you are around at the required times

- Take your time. Don't rush the process of taking photos. Make sure you have the right settings on your camera and that you have composed your image accurately

- Take numerous shots. If possible, take several variations of each shot (change the angle, zoom distance, depth of field)

- Change your settings. Use bracketing to change the exposure either side of what is considered to be correct. This is so that you have differently exposed versions of the same image which can give you greater editing flexibility

- Create your compositions. Take care to actively compose your image, rather than just pointing your camera and hoping

The image on the facing page displays some of the elements noted above. The location was discovered at a time when the light was not suitable so another time had to be selected to capture the image. The composition includes additional elements to add interest to the image (the branch in the top left corner, the fern at the bottom and the red sign to add a color contrast). There is also a natural frame at the top and the island in the background that ensure there is a lot to look at in the photo. Also, several images where taken, some focusing on the individual elements of the composition to give different variations.

Hot tip

When you are taking photos, it is a good idea to do it on your own so that there are no other people there getting annoyed if you are concentrating on taking the best photo.

Assessing Your Work

One of the great advantages of digital photography is that you can instantly review your images, as soon as you have taken them. This is not only useful from a point of view of amending your camera settings, as required, but you can also assess your composition with a view to creating a more effective image.

When you are assessing your work while in the field you should never settle for mediocrity: if you can, also make sure you can get the best image possible, as you never know when you may, or may not, be back at that particular location.

Look at all aspects of an image when you are assessing it: exposure, lighting, focus, color and composition. If you look at this with a critical eye then you will be able to amend your image accordingly when you capture subsequent versions.

> When you are assessing your work while in the field you should never settle for mediocrity

Although a lot of photography is subjective, the concept of assessing your work can be seen in the two images on the facing page. The top image is a perfectly acceptable landscape view. However, if you assess it with a critical eye you may conclude that there is not enough foreground and that the mountain are perhaps too centrally located in the image. By altering the composition by moving the frame slightly to the left the mountains are moved away from the centre of the frame and the shelters take up more of the foreground, while part of the tree is retained at the right border of the image. So by assessing the first image there are now two slightly differing versions of the same shot.

Don't forget

Everyone likes something different in photos and pictures. At the end of the day edit your photos the way that you want and make sure you are happy with them.

Professional Critics

If you want to get a professional view of your images you could send them in to one of the several photography magazines that are available. Most of these contain a section when they review readers' photos. If yours are selected this can be a good way to get a professional opinion.

Varying Distances

Although you usually have to be as static as possible when taking photos, photography should still be viewed as a very mobile hobby. It always pays off to walk around a location to find the best spot or angle for a shot. Also, for individual shots it is also important to vary your distance from the main subject. This can be done either by altering the focal length of your lens, or by physically moving closer or further away from your subject.

When you vary your distance you can get a completely different perspective of a subject. In the two images on the facing page the top one conveys the whole scene, including its context in terms of location and also the people who are involved in the activity. By moving closer to the subject the bottom image displays much more detail of the subject so that it becomes

If you take a collection of shots from differing distances you will be able to build up a narrative about the subject

more like a still life shot. If the distance was increased further from the top shot you would get a much wider context for the shot, although you would then lose some of the detail. If you take a collection of shots from differing distances you will be able to build up a narrative about the subject, showing it from a variety of viewpoints.

When taking shots of people it can be beneficial to be slightly further away from them and use a zoom lens if necessary to get the best shot. This is so you do not crowd them, in which case they may feel more intimidated by the camera and therefore be less relaxed.

If you want to get really close to subjects it is best to use a macro lens, which are designed to be able to focus over very short distances. These are usually more expensive than standard lenses but they are well worth the money if you are going to be doing a lot of close-up photography.

Don't forget

Change your physical distance from subjects as well as using a zoom lens to get a closer shot.

Remember Your Foreground

When considering the composition of a shot, think of the foreground and the background as two separate elements initially and then decide how you can combine the two to create a perfect shot. Try and be as creative as possible and take numerous test shots to see how the final image may look.

The foreground does not have to be the strongest element in an image, but if it is used in this way it can create a powerful statement in your photo. Look at it as an artist building up a canvas: create the foreground and then build the background around it. In the photo on the facing page the flowers produce a strong foreground, not only because of the color contrast with the background, but also because of the angle at which they are shot. This gives the photo an additional perspective rather than just a foreground that is horizontal.

Create Your Own

If you do not have a naturally occurring foreground in your shot, it is perfectly reasonable to add your own. This could be in the form of a prop that you have brought with you or it could just mean moving an item from somewhere else into your shot. However, be careful not to damage any elements of the environment in which you are working.

Foregrounds can also be used effectively to display depth of field: with a large depth of field the foreground and the background should both be in focus; with a shallow depth of field the foreground may be in focus while the background is thrown out of focus. Both of these can be effective techniques and both types of shots should be taken if possible.

Even if the background is the main part of an image, some thought should always be given to the foreground. This can add an extra dimension and make the difference between a good photo and a great one. Also, a foreground element does not have to take up the whole foreground or be in the center of an image. Sometimes a small, subtle, foreground object at the side of the frame can be the element that makes a photo really stand out.

Thinking in Color

It may seem obvious to state that photography is about color, but it is sometimes a simple fact that a lot of people taking photographs forget. Color is always all around us, but when taking photographs it is beneficial to think proactively about color rather than just consider it something that makes up the elements of an image. Some issues to do with color to consider:

- Bands of color. Using separate bands of color (such as the sky and the landscape) can be a great way to highlight the impact of each color

- Color contrasts. Using an object with a color contrast can give a specific focus to an image. For instance, this could be a bright red ball in a green field

196

- Light and color. Color is only as effective as the light shining on it. To experience this, look at the same scene under different lighting conditions. Ideally, lighting should create a reasonable

Ideally, lighting should create a reasonable amount of contrast, in terms of light and shade

amount of contrast, in terms of light and shade, so the full depth of the colors can be seen

- Black and white. Bright colors are not the only way to create effective images. Black and white has traditionally been a favorite option for photographers, as it can create a more atmospheric scene. With digital photography this can be done at the editing stage by converting a colored image into a black and white one. When creating black and white images one of the most important points to remember is to ensure there is enough contrast and shade between the color to give it enough interest and depth

Photographs do not have to be awash with numerous different, vibrant, colors to be effective. The image on the facing page is predominately green, but includes multiple shades and varieties of the color. This gives a richness to the image even though there is only one main color.

The Perfect Portrait

Most photographers like to take photos of people, whether it is portraits of family members or interesting people in different countries or locations.

When you are searching for the perfect portrait there are a few factors that you should keep in mind:

- Ensure the subject is relaxed. This could involve spending more time with them, rather than just turning up and starting to snap away. Talk to your subjects, even while you are capturing your images

- Include interesting objects in the foreground. This could be something related to their work or something that reflects their personality

- Include background objects. These should be used as an additional point of interest, but not be too significant so that it detracts from the main subject.

The portrait below demonstrates some of these points:

14 Editing Techniques

Perfect your Pictures!

Even the best photos can benefit from some

general editing techniques. This chapter

looks at some of these techniques.

Levels

General Editing

The development of digital photography has provided photographers with many advantages. One of these is the ability to edit images on a computer once they have been taken. As far as digital SLR photography is concerned, there are more options for getting better photos when they are first taken. However, they can still benefit from some editing techniques that can be performed reasonably quickly. There are a number of effective image editing programs on the market but the market leader is Adobe Photoshop, which is used for the examples in this chapter. Although there are a much wider range of techniques, those here give an excellent foundation for image editing.

Don't forget

For more detailed information about image editing, have a look at **Photoshop in easy steps** and **Photoshop Elements in easy steps**.

Using Levels

Programs such as Photoshop enable you to change the color range of an image. This is displayed in the Histogram window that displays the tonal range of an image (Window>Histogram).

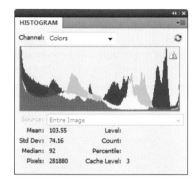

Don't forget

If you drag the slider on the left-hand side of the graph in the Levels window this makes the image darker, if you drag the one on the right-hand side it makes it lighter, and if you drag the middle one this lightens or darkens the midtone colors.

The tonal range can be edited using the Levels function (Image> Adjustments>Levels). This can be used to redistribute pixels between the darkest and lightest points in an image, by dragging the appropriate sliders.

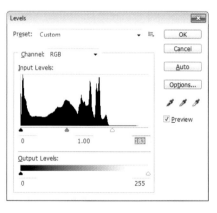

In the images on the facing page, the top one is the original that is slightly dark and under-exposed. By changing the levels the bottom image is much brighter and clearer.

Cropping

Cropping is a technique that can be used to remove unwanted areas of an image and highlight the main subject. The area to be cropped can only be selected as a rectangle. Regardless of how careful you are when you compose an image, it will probably benefit from some cropping, even if it is just to remove the areas around the outside of the image.

Cropping is performed by selecting the Crop tool from the Toolbox.

Click and drag on an image to select the area to be cropped. The area that is selected is retained and the area to be cropped out appears grayed-out

Once the area has been selected, click on the check mark to accept the changes, or the circle to reject them.

In the images on the facing page, the top one is the original image and is acceptable, but once it has been cropped, as in the image below, it becomes a much stronger image as the focus is much more on the canoes. Also, by making the image a different size this also gives it an unusual perspective from a standard image size.

Cloning

Cloning is a technique that can be used to copy one area of an image over another. This can be used to cover up small imperfections in an image, such as a minor blemish or a spot, and also to copy or remove larger items in an image such as a person or an object.

Cloning is performed with the Clone Stamp tool, which can be selected from the Toolbox

Once the Clone Stamp tool has been selected it is used by holding down Alt and then clicking on the part of the image you want to use as the source point. This is the area from where you want the cloning process to start. Then drag the cursor over the area where you want the source area to be copied over. This can be done to copy objects, such as in the image below. Here, the source point is the back of the vehicle on the left. This is then copied at the right-hand side of the image.

Don't forget

To copy an item, keep the cursor held down for the whole time and perform it as one operation. This will ensure that an exact copy of the object is made, rather than cloning from several different areas.

A more common use for cloning is to remove unwanted objects. In the two images on the facing page, the flag from the top image is removed by cloning the areas around it. This is done by selecting several different source points with which to load the Clone Stamp tool. These different areas can then be used to clone over the area of the flag.

When removing an object with cloning it is easiest if it is on a plain background. If the background is more patterned then you will have to use different source points and adopt a step-by-step approach to removing the object.

Selections

One of the most flexible aspects of image editing is the ability to select areas within an image. This can be used in a number of different ways:

- Selecting an object to apply an editing technique to it (such as changing the brightness or contrast) without affecting the rest of the image

- Selecting a particular color in an image

- Selecting an area to apply a special effect to it

- Selecting an area to remove it

There are several tools that cans be used to select areas of an image in different ways.

Marquee tools

These are selection tools that enable you to create symmetrical selections. These are Rectangular and Elliptical as well as single horizontal or vertical line selections.

Lasso tools

These are selection tools that enable you to create asymmetrical selections. These are the Lasso tool, which can be used to make freehand selections, the Polygonal Lasso tool, which can be used to make a selection by creating anchor points like a dot-to-dot picture, and the Magnetic Lasso tool, which can be used to make a selection by identifying the contrast between pixels.

Magic Wand tool

This is a selection tool that can be used to select areas of the same, or similar, color by clicking on areas within an image.

On the facing page the sky in the top image has been selected by clicking on it with the Magic Wand tool. This has then been edited independently from the rest of the image, to give the effect in the bottom image.

Beware

The Lasso tool can be a bit jerky to use and does not make the most accurate selections. The Polygonal Lasso tool is a good option if you want to take your time and create a lot of anchor points and the Magnetic Lasso tool works best when there are two objects of contrasting colors next to each other.

Layers

Layering is a technique that enables you to add additional elements to an image, and place them on separate layers, so that they can be edited and manipulated independently from other elements in the image. It is like creating an image using transparent sheets of film: each layer is independent of the others but, when they are combined, a composite image is created. This is an extremely versatile technique for working with digital images.

Layers are created with the Layers panel (Window>Layers from the Menu bar).

208

New layers can be added by clicking on the Create a New Layer button at the bottom of the Layers panel.

Each new layer is added above the background layer, which always remains on the bottom. The position of additional layers can be moved by dragging them above or below each other.

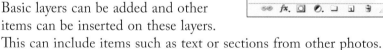

Basic layers can be added and other items can be inserted on these layers. This can include items such as text or sections from other photos.

In addition to basic layers, two other types of layers can be added: fill or adjustment layers. A fill layer is one that adds a colored fill over the layers below it. This can be either a solid color, a gradient or a pattern fill. The top image on the facing page has a gradient fill applied, with the opacity level set to 50% so that the image below can be seen.

An adjustment layer can be used to edit elements such as brightness and contrast, levels and exposure. The bottom image on the facing page has a black and white adjustment layer and it also has a text layer above the adjustment layer.

Filters

Filters can also be thought of as special effects, in terms of what can be applied to a photo. There are a wide range of filter effects, which can be applied from the Filter menu on the Menu bar:

Beware

Use filter effects sparingly because they can become a little over-powering and a little goes a long way.

Hot tip

One excellent filter is Sharpen>Unsharp Mask, which can be used to make the overall appearance of an image seem slightly clearer.

Once a filter effect has been selected, there is a dialog box that can be used to set the properties for the selected filter. Once the properties are selected the filter effect is applied to the image.

215